How
to Overcome
the Darkness

Gary D. Kinnaman is senior pastor of Word of Grace Church in Mesa, Arizona, and author of *Angels Dark and Light*. He has a B.A. from Biola University and an M.A. in theology from Fuller Theological Seminary. Gary and his wife, Marilyn, have three children.

How
to Overcome
the Darkness

Personal Strategies
for Spiritual Warfare

Gary D. Kinnaman

Chosen Books

A Division of Baker Book House Co
Grand Rapids, Michigan 49516

Published by Chosen Books
a division of Baker Book House Company
P.O. Box 6287, Grand Rapids, MI 49516-6287

First printing, March 1999

Previously published by Chosen under the title *Overcoming the Dominion of Darkness*

Printed in the United States of America

Library of Congress Cataloguing-in-Publication Datat

Kinnaman, Gary.
    [Overcoming the dominion of darkness]
    How to overcome the darkness : personal strategies for spiritual warfare /
Gary D. Kinnaman.
     p. cm.
    Originally published: Overcoming the dominion of darkness. c1990.
    Includes bibliographical references and index.
    ISBN 0-8007-9266-1 (pbk.)
    1. Devil. 2. Spiritual warfare. I. Title.
    [BT981.K546 1999]
    235'.4—dc21   98-53435

To my wife,
Marilyn,
for her friendship, love and support

Acknowledgments

A special thanks to Bob Blatter, Chris Wolfard, my associates at Word of Grace, and to Al Ells, Hal Sacks, and Len Griffen, partners in ministry—all friends. I would also like to acknowledge the elders and ministries of Word of Grace for standing with me in the battle. And thanks to Doug Groothuis for reviewing the manuscript and making many helpful suggestions. Without these people, this book would not have been written.

Contents

8 Contents

Part III: The Weapons of Our Warfare
Overcoming the Dominion of Darkness

Foreword

As we step across the threshold from the 1980s to the 1990s and move toward the end of the millennium, momentous changes are taking place before our very eyes. While many of them can be pinpointed in the realms of international politics, medicine, space travel, global economics, electronics and others, none is more significant than changes taking place in the spiritual realm. Quite obviously, God is doing new and amazing things through His people and through His Church.

How to Overcome the Darkness is clearly a book for the 1990s. Gary Kinnaman was hearing from God as he was writing the book. What you are about to read is a significant part of what the Spirit is saying to the churches these days. Never before in living memory has the Christian Church, across denominational and regional lines, been so ready to learn about and engage in spiritual warfare. This book, in my opinion, is a vital resource for those God is calling to go to the front lines, both for those who are just beginning and for those who have been there before.

My friend Gary Kinnaman is uniquely equipped to produce this resource for active Christians across the board. He is the pastor of a large, dynamic, growing church in the Phoenix metropolitan area. As such he is in constant touch with ordinary people. He knows what they think, where they hurt and how to help them. He is also a trainer of pastors and a personal counselor to many. He knows both their strengths and their vulnerabilities. Gary is a scholar. He has not shied away from academia, from an analytical mind, from compiling bibliographies, from building a library or from using the Greek in Bible study. As you read this book you will see that he is conversant with the opinions of scholars from across the ecclesiastical spectrum.

But more important than being a pastor, a teacher and a scholar, Gary Kinnaman is a practitioner. He does not write about something he learned from books or lectures. Hands-on spiritual warfare is part of his regular ministry activities. By this I do not mean that he "sees a demon behind every bush," as some might fear just from reading the title of the book. In fact he writes wisely, "If there is a danger in spiritual warfare, it is giving the devil too much attention." There is great balance in this book. Kinnaman, himself a charismatic Christian, is not at all sectarian. I do not know of another book I could recommend more highly to my non-charismatic colleagues.

Several books on spiritual warfare are available, but I have two general observations on them. For one thing we do not have enough of them. Some of us who are seeing the signs of the times moving toward the year 2000 believe that our spiritual warfare in the next few years will be extremely intense. We Christians need all the help and collective wisdom we can get as we move forward under the Lordship of Jesus Christ. More resources like this are needed.

My second observation is that some of the books on spiritual warfare (but certainly not all of them) are not as helpful as they could be. It is not my purpose to discredit them, for most all of them contain some excellent insights. But I must admit that some of them cause me concern, make me uneasy. *Overcoming the Dominion of Darkness* is not one of these. It is my kind of book, written with an enviable combination of grace and power.

If you have enjoyed *This Present Darkness* or *Piercing the Darkness*, you are ready to go from fiction to fact and deepen your understanding of the ways God's Kingdom is invading the kingdom of evil in our days. There is no better guide for doing this than the book you have in your hands.

C. Peter Wagner
Fuller Theological Seminary
Pasadena, California

Preface

There is a critical need for practical theology of spiritual warfare. Our materialistic world view has relegated demons and supernatural power to a more primitive time in human history. The American Church is willing to accept demonization on the mission field, but here at home our belief in the power of darkness is academic.

But this is changing. The New Age movement has brought a new awareness to the Church that there is a spiritual dimension teeming with dark beings. Charismatics, of course, have been talking about these things for some time, but the evangelical community, possessing a basic mistrust of subjective experience, has been wary.

Recently, a new Christian novel, *This Present Darkness*, has become a bestseller. A kind of modern *Screwtape Letters*, it has had a profound effect on those who have read it. But it is fiction. When I first began thinking about writing this book, I asked the bookbuyer for a large Christian bookstore if he could recommend any serious books on spiritual warfare. He could not think of any.

As a result of my research for this book, I have discovered that actually quite a bit of writing on the subject has been done. Most of it, however, spotlights the more sensational, albeit real aspects of demonization and the occult.

This book is different. I have come to believe that every Christian, sooner or later, will have a notable close encounter of the dark kind. Furthermore, life's days are filled with ordinary, natural events that may have extraordinary, supernatural origins. Every believer must be properly trained to recognize, resist and overcome his or her spiritual enemies. I have attempted to present a biblically balanced, sensible and practical guide to help you understand spiritual warfare, Satan's schemes and God's counterstrategies.

One other point: Some readers may feel that my interpretation of the armor of God is fanciful. Did the apostle Paul, when he listed the full armor of God in Ephesians 6, really have in mind all the things I have discussed in my five lengthy chapters? Probably not. Yet I believe that the full armor—truth, righteousness, peace, salvation and faith—suggests major categories of spiritual truth, an understanding of which is necessary for the Christian to resist the devil.

Those of us who serve together on the staff of our church, Word of Grace in Mesa, Arizona, have prayed for every reader of this book. We have prayed for you—that you will have your spiritual senses awakened, and that God will strengthen you with power through His Spirit in your inner being (Ephesians 3:16).

Part I
War on the Saints

Recognizing the Dominion of Darkness

1
Rediscovering the Spiritual Dimension

Our struggle is not against flesh and blood, but
against the rulers, against the authorities, against the
powers of this dark world and against the spiritual
forces of evil in the heavenly realms.

Ephesians 6:12

It was a crucial vote. Pro-life leaders had carefully prepared new legislation to be presented to the Arizona
House of Representatives. It had been announced at a
public rally that this proposed law, House Bill 2088 (1988),
was designed to become a test case for the Supreme Court
to reconsider Roe v. Wade. Pro-life forces had selected
Arizona, we were told, because of the likelihood that this
kind of legislation would pass.

A friend of mine, David Everitt, the Director of the Crisis Pregnancy Centers of Arizona, and other pro-life leaders had talked with every representative. Passage was
assured by one vote. But on the day of the vote there was
a delay in the legislative process, and the legislator with
the deciding vote, Jim Ratliff, suddenly became ill and had
to leave the Capitol building—fifteen minutes before the
roll call. The House voted in his absence, and the bill failed
by one vote.

Because of the unusual circumstances, however, the bill was allowed to be reintroduced a few days later and a second vote was taken. Once again the pro-life bloc was certain of success. But at the last moment, to everyone's astonishment, one of the "certain" yes votes, Sterling Ridge, suddenly and unexpectedly changed his mind. The legislation to protect unborn children failed again by one vote.

Coincidental? Was this legislative decision merely the consequence of a complex set of circumstances? Or was this a significant human event that had been somehow influenced by negative spiritual forces?

Some years ago I was working as an associate pastor in a church that had a large radio ministry. We owned a Compugraphic electronic typesetter, obsolete now but technologically advanced for that time. One day, our secretary was preparing typeset transcripts for the publication of the radio broadcast when something curious began to occur. The printer would not respond to her entries. All she could get was some garbled words about Satan and demons.

She called the staff together, and we all stared in disbelief at the unusual document. Then someone proposed the unlikely solution that we pray for the machine. We did and the problem disappeared.

Coincidental? Perhaps. Weird? Yes. Providential? We did not think the malfunction was the "perfect will of God," because we prayed against the problem, corrected the copy and printed the right message. Could this have been a "spiritual" problem?

In the hundreds of hours I have spent in front of a word processor, my computer has only glitched twice: once when I had just finished writing a pamphlet on deliverance from spiritual oppression, and once when I was writing material on the absolute Lordship of Christ. In each case, my computer jammed inexplicably, and I lost all the material. Coincidental?

A few months ago I entered my office through the private door. Unknown to me, one of our counselors was using my office for a premarital counseling session. The couple was having serious problems. At that very moment, just before I stepped in, they had both broken into a violent rage. When they saw me, "the pastor," their demeanor changed instantly! But they were still steaming inside. I sat down to speak with them for a few moments, and their terrible anger began to re-emerge.

Talking was not helping. I recognized that this was a "spiritual" problem and began to pray. This time, it was the presence of God, not my pastoral charisma, that literally changed the atmosphere. I stepped out of the office, and our counselor continued the session. Later, we shared our jubilation over the incredible timing of my "unplanned" interruption of her session, and of the dramatic change that took place when we prayed.

Was all of this coincidental? Not likely. Providential? No doubt. Was it spiritual warfare? Is it possible that dark forces can have a subtle but powerful influence on marriages and families?

I was late one evening for an important meeting of our governing board. When I walked into the meeting, I could feel something very uncomfortable in the room. Two of our key members were discussing an important issue, but their conversation was going nowhere. Everyone in the room seemed confused. I was confused.

Then I realized that another member of our board, who was relatively silent, was very unhappy about some decisions we were making. His demeanor and his brief but barbed comments seemed to be affecting the spirit of the entire meeting. *This is a spiritual problem*, I said to myself.

Oddly enough, churches do not often recognize that their problems have spiritual roots, so we argue more and pray less. I have done it myself. But this time I prayed—silently but fervently. And the spirit of the meeting took a decided turn for the better. A coincidence? Not likely. Spiritual warfare? I am convinced that our meeting was being eroded by a disruptive spirit. Principalities and powers of darkness are commissioned to affect governments, destroy families and friendships and even influence church leaders in order to disrupt the work of the Kingdom of God.

Have you ever considered this possibility? Have you been in the midst of a trial that you could not seem to overcome even though there was no logical reason for it? Have you wondered about verses in the Bible about powers of evil, the "rulers of darkness"? If you have, then I believe you will find answers here you have been seeking. We can learn to repel the enemy's invading darkness and stand securely in the light.

If you have been skeptical about this area of religious belief you are not alone, but I think you will come to see that the realm of darkness is not only real, it is active in the affairs of God's people.

The Prevailing World View?

"We wrestle not against flesh and blood." Most Christians believe this because it is in the Bible, but most do not live as though they believe it. C. Fred Dickason, chairman of the theology department at Moody Bible Institute, writes in his book *Demon Possession and the Christian*:

A believer may discount the spirit world and consider that certain occult activities are but games and that demons attacking Christians directly is just superstition. Christianity, after all, rules out superstition. [Thus,] he fails to see the reality of the occult and the dangers of sin, and rules out spiritual warfare with the possibility of demonization (p. 230).

Christians are often ignorant of spiritual warfare, because we have been unwittingly seduced into accepting a secular, humanistic world view, something the German theologian Dietrich Bonhoeffer called "the world come of age," a world without God.

In one of his famous "papers from prison," written in confinement in a Nazi cell, Bonhoeffer wrote a concise but penetrating analysis of the emerging godlessness of our age. About a movement that began more or less in the thirteenth century, he observed that "man has learned to deal with himself in all questions of importance without recourse to 'the working hypothesis' called 'God' . . . everything gets along without God" (*Letters and Papers from Prison*, p. 324). The evil of our age is not its antagonism toward God, but its indifference.

We Christians readily admit our faith in a real God and even believe in a "personal" devil, but we are woefully unaware of Satan's devices. An older relative of mine, who has been a committed Christian since childhood, asked me sincerely, "What is spiritual warfare?" We cannot fight if we are ignorant of the battle raging around us. In spiritual battles ignorance is impotence.

Merrill Unger, renowned Bible scholar and former professor of Old Testament at Dallas Theological Seminary, wrote in *Demons in the World Today:*

Are demons interacting with our modern world of science and so-called enlightenment? Skepticism and ignorance concerning the Word of God produce appalling misapprehensions of reality. Men who deny the existence of Satan and demons betray their rejection of biblical teachings; people who deny the activity of demons in contemporary life betray their ignorance of significant portions of the Bible (p. 17).

Every circumstance in life has a cause: God, the devil, natural forces, me—or all of the above in an intricate blend. Many things in life are undoubtedly coincidental, or are the general consequence of sin. But many are not. It takes spiritual sensitivity to discern the natural and supernatural influences behind the events of life. I am wary of "superspiritual" Christians who see a demon in everyone and everything, but I am equally cautious around sincere Christians who do not embrace the biblical world view that harmonizes the supernatural with ordinary events.

Once the disciples of Jesus were terrified by the wind and waves of a sudden, violent storm on the Sea of Galilee. Jesus did something most Christians would never consider: He rebuked the weather! This shows not only that the Creator Himself was incarnate in the Man Christ Jesus, but also that the ultimate power in life is spiritual, not natural.

In the Old Testament weather patterns were rarely seen as chance events, but were understood by *spiritual* application as signs of God's blessing or disfavor. And in the New Testament, a large proportion of the recorded physical healings involved deliverance from a *spirit* of infirmity.

Are these merely expressions of a more primitive and superstitious time? Or are there forces at work we have not reckoned with?

What we have before us is a titanic clash between the biblical world view, which integrates the natural power of God's world and the supernatural powers at work in it, over against the modern secular world view, which in its godlessness has excised spirituality altogether.

Our celebrated news media are a good example of a secular world view that has prevailed with great impact on all of us. Their view of the world has been not only non-Christian, but completely non-spiritual. Only rarely has the pattern been broken. Several years ago *Time* reported on the Christianity and spirituality of Cory Aquino, and how her prayer life may have led to peaceful political change in the Philippines.

More recently, the press reluctantly but openly reported the spiritual power behind Dave Dravecky's comeback from cancer to pitch again for the San Francisco Giants. One reporter, in an editorial on the sports page of the Portland *Oregonian* (August 12, 1989), admitted that something had happened, but he was not sure if it was Jesus, Buddha or Reese's Peanut Butter Cups.

This secularization of society has deeply influenced the Church for generations. Belief in demons and the supernatural power of God has become academic.

But I believe this is changing. We are starting to see a resurgence of religion—particularly in the non-Christian realm. This is apparent in the rise in interest in cults, the occult and especially the New Age movement, which offers a rediscovery of basic human spirituality and the authenticity of the spiritual dimension. New Agers believe in spiritual power—albeit the wrong kind. I am convinced that the New Age has become so popular in the West because of the spiritual vacuum of our predominantly secular world view, even in the Church. The Church has generally failed to provide people with genuine encounters with the power of God.

F. LaGuard Smith, professor of law at Pepperdine University and author of *Out on a Broken Limb,* was interviewed about his thoughtful Christian response to the New Age. Why, he was asked in the March/April 1989 issue of *The Wittenburg Door,* are New Agers so fascinated with the bizarre? He responded:

> All the New Agers are really saying is that there is a spiritual dimension which exists and that we ought to be tuned in to it. The strange thing is, we Christians have believed that all along. We *should* have believed that all along. The problem is that modern Christians are very religious, but they don't have a clue about spiritual things. . . . We have forgotten that . . . there is a battle going on.

Orthodoxy is necessary, but it is not enough. If it is true that our battle is not against flesh and blood, then we need spiritual insight and power of our own to make a fight of it. Correct doctrine—as necessary as it is for the long-term stability of the Church—is not adequate to bring down the legions of spiritual darkness arrayed against her. While carefully defined truth is necessary to confront and overcome error, we must realize that error does not exist merely in the intellect.

Why is it so difficult to share the true Christ with someone who is in a cult? Because we are facing a stalwart spirit of religious deception. When a Mormon, for example, is caught in a doctrinal corner, he will always fall back on his "testimony," a powerfully convincing, personal spiritual experience that assures him beyond a doubt that Mormonism is the only true religion. This kind of spiritual power cannot be broken with a convincing presentation of Christianity alone.

Christianity is not just the only correct world religion. Correct words alone will not win the battle. Christianity is the power of the Kingdom of God against the power of the kingdom of darkness. Paul wrote, "Our gospel came to you not simply with words, but also with power, with the Holy Spirit" (1 Thessalonians 1:5). This theme is repeated in 1 Corinthians 2:4: "My message and my preaching were not with wise and persuasive words, but with a demonstration of the Spirit's power." The Church in the West has a form of godliness, but we are guilty of denying its power (see 2 Timothy 3:5).

Only in the last 25 years has the Church in the West begun to awaken to her need for the special presence and power of God. And only within the last decade has there been an emerging awareness of spiritual warfare.

Friends of mine, Doug and Becky Groothuis, are dedicated to a ministry of unmasking and confronting the New Age movement. Doug, who has published two bestselling books on the subject, is uncompromisingly orthodox and has an unwavering commitment to meticulous research.

He is not easily persuaded by emotional, subjective experiences, but through his careful study of the New Age, Doug has personally discovered the realities of the spiritual dimension. Asking for prayer, Doug and Becky have told me about a dark cloud of personal oppression and direct satanic interference with their ministry.

Becky wrote to me in a recent letter, "Writing [Doug's third book exposing distorted views of Christ] has been itself a living lesson in spiritual warfare. There truly is no book like this on the market, and Satan has been leveling his big guns at both of us for the past year in an effort to keep it that way." Prayer for one another is not only our Christian duty; sometimes it is a matter of life and death. Spiritual warfare is serious business, and prayer is essential.

What About Spiritual Forces?

Charles Kraft, author and professor of anthropology and intercultural communication at Fuller Theological Seminary,* describes how his failures on the mission field led him to spiritual renewal and a healing ministry. In an article entitled "Shifting World Views, Shifting Attitudes" (*Equipping the Saints*, September/October 1987, p. 10), Kraft recounts how he was raised a "typical" evangelical. He was well-trained in biblical studies, anthropology and linguistics. He writes,

> We were well-prepared [for the mission field]—except, as it turned out, in the area the Nigerians considered the most important: their relationships with the spirit world. These spirits, they told me, cause disease, accidents and death, hinder fertility of people, animals and fields, bring drought, destroy relationships, and harass the innocent. But I could not help these people, for I was just plain ignorant in this area.

"This area," the Nigerian belief that spiritual forces influence the events of daily life, is not unlike the teaching of the Bible that the spiritual realm is a key factor in our lives—that there is spiritual force bent on our destruction and the spiritual power of God to subdue it.

* Charles Kraft has recently published the book *Christianity with Power* (Ann Arbor, Mich.: Servant, 1989) on this matter of world views and how they affect our thinking as Christians. I recommend it.

The importance of recognizing the true, biblical world view was reaffirmed by another acquaintance. Paul, born in India, came to the United States in the late 1960s for training at a respected seminary. He graduated with a master of divinity degree and returned to India to open a mission. His initial work proved to be fruitless. He realized that his American education did not prepare him to confront the spiritual darkness in his country.

So he and his associates agreed to fast, pray and seek God for the power of Pentecost. Almost immediately, their ministry began to witness phenomenal results. Since that time, more than 40,000 people have been baptized, and they have established some 1,500 churches and home Bible training centers. Paul invited me to go to India with him. "You have not experienced the supernatural," he explained, "until you visit my country. Come, and you will never be the same."

Our secularized world view is a veil concealing the supernatural—both good and bad—and rendering us powerless in spiritual conflict. The apostle Paul wrote to the Ephesians,

> I keep asking that the God of our Lord Jesus Christ, the glorious Father, may give you the Spirit of wisdom *and revelation*. . . . I pray also that *the eyes of your heart* [your spiritual discernment and perception] *may be enlightened* in order that you may know . . . his incomparably great power for us who believe.
>
> Ephesians 1:17–19

Just this week, after I began writing this chapter, one of the elders in our church, Carl, greeted me Sunday morning and told me about his frightening experience the night before. At two in the morning, he and his wife, Dee, were startled from their sleep by a ferocious banging and crashing at their front door.

Dee ran to the phone to call the police, while Carl approached the door cautiously to negotiate with the madman who continued pounding and yelling obscenities. After no little hollering back and forth, Carl understood the man to say that someone had broken the windshield of his car, and he was convinced the culprit was in Carl's house.

The police were slow in arriving, and suddenly it occurred to Carl that he should pray! He reported this to me in a kind of disbelief that he had not thought of calling on God until that moment. But when Carl cried out to the Lord and appealed to the authority of Christ over whatever spiritual power was controlling the man, within *one minute* the intruder had left and disappeared from the neighborhood!

Spiritual blindness leads to spiritual powerlessness. We are ignorant of the devil's devices, and this is precisely his scheme, to keep us that way. My prayer is that your eyes will be opened so you will see the spiritual dimension more clearly. And my prayer is that you will lay claim to the immeasurably great power given to us who believe. It is the very same power, as Paul writes, that raised Christ from the dead and placed Him above every throne and dominion (Ephesians 1:20–23). Jesus is Lord, and the Church is God's revelation of the Lordship of Christ in a world caught in the devices of the devil—snared but not lost, as the Christians who enter the battle will see.

2
Signs of the Times

And the fifth angel sounded [the trumpet] . . . and he opened the bottomless pit; and there arose a smoke out of the pit . . . and there came out of the smoke locusts . . . and their torment was as the torment of a scorpion.   Revelation 9:1–3, 5, KJV

I was having lunch recently with two colleagues in ministry. One has done extensive missionary work behind the Iron Curtain, and the other, a former music minister, is now a writer for a major publisher of Christian music.

I was telling them about a crisis time in the ministry of our church. It was a story with a familiar ring for those who have been in Christian work for any length of time. Misunderstanding. Broken relationships. Hurt and pain for everyone.

To my surprise, one of my two friends interpreted my experience in a way quite uncharacteristic of his denominational persuasion. He had read reports, he told me, of Satan worshipers who had targeted key ministries with their "prayers," and had even infiltrated Christian services from time to time in order to disrupt them. He felt that our church's experience could well have been caused by such an attack.

As we are rediscovering the reality of the spiritual dimension and spiritual warfare, we will recognize it more and more as a sign of the times. The Bible gives every indication that the closer we come to the return of Christ, the more the battle is going to heat up. In fact, the unprecedented advance of the Church in the last part of the twentieth century, the resurgence of apostolic-like signs and wonders, and the rising consciousness of spiritual warfare are as much a sign of the nearness of the Lord's return as many of the geopolitical events in the Middle East.

Mark Bubeck, a graduate of Talbot Seminary and author of the bestselling book, *The Adversary*, writes, "Believers are being jolted awake in the reality of their participation in a spiritual warfare. This warfare promises to intensify as the return of our Lord draws near" (p. 15). With this in mind, let's consider several important prophetic chapters in the Bible.

Revelation 13: The Beast

Revelation 13 is one of several passages that point to a flood of spiritual and moral evil in the last days. This apocalyptic chapter describes a great and terrible beast rising from the sea. By the description that follows, it is evident that we are reading about the rise of the Antichrist, the final, global challenge to the Kingdom of God before Christ comes again.

"The sea" in verse 1 is thought by many to be a symbol of the earth's billions, in tumult like the waves of a raging ocean. Out of this sea of humanity emerges a face of terror, a hideous creature with seven heads and ten horns. "The whole world was astonished and followed the beast" (verse 3).

But beyond the adulation given the beast, "men worshiped the dragon because he had given authority to the beast" (verse 4). The zenith of worldly power and evil will be directly empowered by Satan himself, and the focus of this force will be to establish the devil's reign on the earth. This he will do by giving the beast "power to make war against the saints" (verse 7).

If you are a Christian, then you are a specific target of spiritual darkness. Satan knows that you hold the keys of heaven. As a citizen of the Kingdom of the Most High God, you are standing in the way of Satan's ultimate objective: the destruction of every Christian and actual "authority over every tribe, people, language and nation" (verse 7). Satan wants total control over every human being on the face of the earth.

Bible scholars have debated the identity of the Antichrist, and some believe that he will not be revealed until after the Rapture of the Church. My purpose is not to outline these finer points of Bible prophecy, but to highlight the obvious: *The last days will be characterized by an unprecedented attack against the people of God and their Christ.* Don't ignore it. Don't downplay it. There has been a declaration of war on the saints.

The symbolism of Revelation 13 echoes the prophet Daniel's description of the same events.* Both passages use the symbols of the ten horns (Revelation 13:1; Daniel 7:20) and a mouth that speaks boastfully (Revelation 13:5; Dan-

---

* When I was working on the first draft of this chapter, I decided to take a break at this point in the manuscript. Before storing the document on my word processor, I always run a spelling check, which also gives me a word count for the document. The word count to this point in the chapter, remarkably, was 666! This may be nothing more than an odd coincidence, but the chance of this occurring, on this particular chapter on the Antichrist, was too unusual to leave unnoted. Dietrich Bonhoeffer once wrote that miracles always remain a mystery. The believer sees a sign. The unbeliever sees nothing.

iel 7:20), and mention war on the saints (Revelation 13:7; Daniel 7:21). Both Daniel and John predict, as a sign of the end times, a spiritual conflict of unprecedented intensity.

The growing interest in spiritual warfare in our generation is a prophetic signpost indicating that the Kingdom of God is at hand. The Church is rediscovering the powerful message of the Kingdom,* and Satan is resisting the saints with unrivaled fury. But the gates of hell will not prevail! "The kingdom of the world [will] become the kingdom of our Lord and of his Christ, and he will reign for ever and ever" (Revelation 11:15).

The end will finally come "when [Christ will hand] over the kingdom to God the Father after he has destroyed all dominion, authority and power." In the meantime, "he must reign until he has put all his enemies under his feet" (1 Corinthians 15:24–25), and the saints will play an active role in all of this. God has appointed Christ "to be head over everything for the church, which is his body, the fullness of him who fills everything in every way" (Ephesians 1:22–23). The Church is Christ present in the world. God has purposed that now, in this age, His manifold wisdom and power will be made known to the rulers and authorities in the heavenly realms *through the Church* (Ephesians 3:10–11).

Daniel 2: The Great Statue

This is also the underlying message of Nebuchadnezzar's prophetic vision in Daniel 2, a panorama of the fu-

* In a recent publication, *Foresight: Ten Major Trends that Will Dramatically Affect the Future of the Church,* Christian futurist Howard Snyder acknowledged an emerging interest in the Kingdom theme. He predicts that the Church in the next few decades will continue to move away from institutional tradition to Kingdom theology.

ture. Nebuchadnezzar, the king of Babylon, dreamed a dream. He awakened terrified, but he could not remember what he dreamed. Tormented, the king called for his magicians to interpret his nightmare, but no one had a clue as to what the king had dreamed, let alone what it meant.

But Daniel had the wisdom of the true God, and was given both the dream and its interpretation: "You looked, O king, and there before you stood a large statue . . . awesome in appearance" (Daniel 2:31). Daniel described the image: It had a head of gold, chest and arms of silver, abdomen and thighs of bronze, legs of iron and feet of iron mixed with clay. Each of these elements has been identified by Bible scholars as representative of specific ancient kingdoms. In the broader sense, however, the statue represents the world system in any age. It is dazzling like gold on the face of things, but its foundation is riddled with weakness. The outward success of the world is a grand delusion.

Out of the blue, Daniel continued, a rock not cut with human hands (a symbol of purely divine power) struck the image at its weakest point—its feet, a common biblical symbol of authority (see Psalm 8:6, 110:1; 1 Corinthians 15:24–25). Thus we see that the divine authority of the Rock, Jesus Christ, destroys the demonic authority of human kingdoms.

Daniel explained, "The God of heaven will set up a kingdom that will never be destroyed, nor will it be left to another people. It will crush all those kingdoms and bring them to an end, but it will itself endure forever. This is the meaning of the vision of the rock cut out of a mountain" (Daniel 2:44–45). The authority base of the kingdoms of this world is Satan himself, and Jesus Christ came to destroy the works of the devil.

One more thing: "The rock that struck the statue became a huge mountain and filled the whole earth" (Daniel 2:35). How does a rock become a mountain? By reproducing itself! How does a rock reproduce itself? Peter wrote, "As you come to him, the living Stone . . . you also, like living stones, are being built into a spiritual house" (1 Peter 2:4).

As Jesus' flesh was the temple and dwelling place of the Most High God (John 2:19–21), so the Church is the dwelling place of the presence of Christ. God was in the world in Jesus, and Satan tried unsuccessfully to destroy Him. Jesus is in the world in us and has given us a Kingdom commission, so Satan has redirected his hostility toward us.

Nebuchadnezzar's vision, according to Daniel, "will take place in the future" (Daniel 2:45). A parallel passage is Isaiah 2:2: *"In the last days* the mountain [high place, Kingdom power]* of the Lord's temple will be established as chief among the mountains [high places, kingdom powers]."

The Rock will become a great mountain, a high place and stronghold of God's Kingdom filling the whole earth. The Rock is Christ. The great mountain is the Church, living stones, reproductions of Christ through the new birth. But Satan will not take this lying down. He will put up the fight of his life, equaled only by his attempt to kill Jesus and keep Him in the grave.

Revelation 9: This Present Darkness

The last days will be characterized by a flood of demonic power, evil and wickedness, which brings us back to our introductory verse: "And the fifth angel sounded . . . and

---

* In the next chapter I explain how "mountain" is often used in the Bible as a figure of speech for Kingdom authority.

he opened the bottomless pit; and there arose a smoke out of the pit . . . and there came out of the smoke locusts . . . and their torment was as the torment of a scorpion" (Revelation 9:1–3, 5, KJV). In the last days, the pit of hell will be opened to release a terrible, dark cloud of spiritual evil.

At first glance, the image here is of a black stormcloud of locusts, one of the most feared plagues of the ancient world. The prophet Joel in the Old Testament received a similar prophetic last-days vision in which a hoard of locusts is unleashed against the people of God. The hoard is referred to as an army in chapter 2: "A large and mighty army comes. . . . They all march in line, not swerving from their course" (verses 2, 7).

A closer look at Revelation 9, however, reveals that these are no ordinary locusts. They have the power to torment like scorpions (Revelation 9:10). Following the biblical symbol of serpents and scorpions as representative of demons (see Luke 10:19), this cloud of scorpion-like locusts is in fact "this present darkness" (Ephesians 6:12, AMPLIFIED), the "spiritual forces of evil." And "they had as king over them the angel of the Abyss, whose name in Hebrew is Abaddon, and in Greek, Apollyon"—the "destroyer," the prince of darkness (Revelation 9:11).

2 Thessalonians 2: The Man of Sin

The apostle Paul wrote of the same event in slightly different terms. The unveiling of the Antichrist, the man of sin, would occur in the last days, when "the one who now holds it back," whom I take to mean the Holy Spirit, lifts the restraint (2 Thessalonians 2:7). When that happens, when the abyss is opened, the "lawless one" will be revealed. Along with this, the world will see "the work of

Satan displayed in all kinds of counterfeit miracles, signs and wonders, and in every sort of evil that deceives those who are perishing" (2 Thessalonians 2:9–10). In the last days, "this present darkness" will grow darker still.

If the opening of the abyss of demonic influence and power will characterize the end times, we must expect an accompanying tidal wave of religious deception, just as Jesus Himself predicted. "What will be the sign of your coming and of the end of the age?" the disciples asked Jesus. "Watch out," the Lord replied, "that no one deceives you. *For many will come in my name,* claiming 'I am the Christ,' and will deceive many" (Matthew 24:3–5). Here, in what is known as the Lord's Olivet Discourse, religious deception is the *first* warning signal of the end of the world. Verses 10, 11 and 24 describe subsequent apostasy, false prophets and deceptive signs and miracles.

Paul echoed these words as he warned his young disciple Timothy, "The Spirit clearly says that in later times some will abandon the faith and follow deceiving spirits and things taught by demons" (1 Timothy 4:1). We are nearing the end of the twentieth century, and the secularization of society is beginning to fade. Humanity with all of its science and technology is not getting less religious, but more. God-is-dead is dead.

Our responsibility, then, is to watch and pray, so that the Day of the Lord does not startle us like a thief in the night. We must also be self-controlled and alert, because the Day of the Lord is preceded by the day of the devil. "Watch out that no one deceives you," Jesus said. "See, I have told you ahead of time" (Matthew 24:4, 25).

Paul wrote in a second letter to Timothy, "In view of [Jesus'] appearing and his kingdom, I give you this charge: . . . *Be prepared.* . . . For the time will come when men will not put up with sound doctrine. Instead, to suit their own desires, they will gather around them a great number of teachers to say what their itching ears want to hear" (2 Timothy 4:1–3).

Gullibility! Spiritual deception begins when we refuse to submit to anyone's authority but our own, when we are without structure and without standards. Spiritually naïve people are vulnerable not only to enticing teaching, but to the control of the spiritual darkness behind that teaching. In contrast, being teachable means we are submitted to proper authority. Teachable does not mean just being open, but being open with caution.

Gullibility is openness without restraint, listening to whatever we want, to whatever pleases our spiritual fancy. The problem is, what makes us feel good now may make us feel terrible later! If spiritual deception is a sign of the times, then our correct, calculated response must be to watch, pray and search the Scriptures carefully (see Acts 17:11).

How to Recognize Spiritual Deception

At this point it is important to identify common denominators of religious deception. Most of these will be found in every cult or aberrant religious group.

One: A Deviation from Orthodoxy

Orthodox is derived from two Greek words that mean "correct opinion" or "straight thinking." When we speak of the orthodox doctrines of the Christian faith, we are referring to beliefs that have been generally accepted by the mainstream of the Church throughout her history. The essential Christian doctrines include the following:

The Bible. The Bible alone is the source of divine revelation. It is the very Word of God, verbally inspired in the original Hebrew and Greek, complete in its revelation and without errors in its statements.

The Trinity. The traditional belief of Christianity, given here in the wording of the Westminster Catechism, is that "there are three persons in the Godhead; the Father, the Son, and the Holy Ghost; and these three are one God, the same in substance, equal in power and glory."

Jesus Christ. "What do you think about the Christ?" (Matthew 22:42). More than anything else, the answer to this question will unveil the rightness or wrongness of a religious sect. More often than not, a cult will have a deviant view of the Person of Jesus Christ.

Christians believe that Jesus was fully God and fully man, God made flesh. He was not "a" god, nor was He merely a man. He was crucified for the sins of the world and on the third day rose, literally, from the dead. He has ascended into heaven and is seated at the right hand of the throne of God. A person (or group) in spiritual deception will often claim he has found an alternative way to God. He disputes the words of our Lord Jesus, "I am the way and the truth and the life. No one comes to the Father except through me" (John 14:6).

Man. All men are sinners by nature and by practice, are sentenced to eternal separation from God and are in need of personal regeneration by faith in the shed blood of the Lord Jesus Christ.

Salvation. Salvation is by grace, a free gift of God, through faith in the Lord Jesus Christ. Salvation is not earned by good works, although good works will be the fruit of a regenerate life.

The Second Coming. Christ will return personally and

bodily to judge both the living and the dead. All those whose names are not found in the Lamb's Book of Life will be cast into the lake of fire for eternal punishment. The saints will spend eternity with the Lord.

Two: A Redefinition of Terms

In his chapter "Scaling the Language Barrier" in *Kingdom of the Cults*, Walter Martin wrote,

> The average non-Christian cult owes its very existence to the fact that it has utilized the terminology of Christianity, has borrowed liberally from the Bible, almost always out of context, and has sprinkled its format with evangelical clichés and terms wherever possible or advantageous. . . . On encountering a cultist, then, always remember that you are dealing with a person who is familiar with Christian terminology, and who has carefully redefined it to fit the system of thought he or she now embraces (p. 20).

Three: Special Revelation

Almost without exception, deception begins with a claim to some special revelation outside and beyond the Bible. This may be as "sophisticated" as the Book of Mormon, or as simple but equally binding as the unique teachings of a religious group's leader. The group may even be quasi-Christian, but its understanding of the Bible is based more on what the leader says about the Bible; his word becomes the standard for the group or organization.

A fundamental principle of Mormon theology is that God's special revelation to man did not end with the Bible. The irony of this kind of thinking is that special revelation does not ultimately set apart Mormonism from any other cult. Special revelation simply lumps Mormonism with all of the other unorthodox systems of belief. I once asked a Mormon why the Book of Mormon was more correct than the *Watchtower* magazine of the Jehovah's Witnesses, or the revelations of the "Reverend" Moon and his Unification Church. He could not answer. They *all* claim special revelation! Either they are all right, or they are all wrong.

Four: Exclusiveness

We could call this the I-am-absolutely-right, you-are-absolutely-wrong mentality. Admittedly, even in the Christian mainstream there are doctrinal differences, and some denominations are more "narrow" in their views and less tolerant of dissimilarities. But in the final analysis, there is a basic recognition among true Christians that the universal Body of Christ goes beyond denominational differences.

The ultimate issue is one's relationship with Christ, not one's membership in a particular religious sect. But members of cults never see it that way. Everyone else is wrong. The tragedy of Jonestown, where hundreds of people committed suicide at the whim of their guru, is a supreme example of exclusiveness.

Five: Closemindedness

I once conversed with a minister of a small church falling over the borderline of orthodox Christianity. Its teachings were cult-like. During our discussion I asked him if he knew the definition of a particular New Testament Greek term relevant to our discussion. I'll never forget his response. He literally whirled around in scorn and hissed, "You people are so dumb." A rational discussion was impossible, and he demonstrated an absolute intolerance of my views.

Six: Legalism

In order to protect their exclusiveness, in order to remain isolated, cultists must develop their own set of special rules, which their followers must obey. Strict obedience is necessary to feel the love of the leader and the group, and even to get to heaven! Tragically, I have even seen this kind of legalism implied in Christian churches, where departing individuals or families are given the impression that they are out of the will of God by leaving, and therefore under God's judgment. This is not Christian; it is cultic and demonic.

In this sense the teachings of the cults are, at their roots, based on law, not grace. The fundamental message of salvation by grace alone distinguishes Christianity from every other religious system. The Gospel is unique. It is "good news" because God has taken the initiative in salvation. Technically, no one ever "finds" the Lord. Jesus is the One who came both *to seek and to save* the lost (see Luke 19:10). Cults are always law-oriented, and they redefine grace to suit their systems.

Whenever you are speaking with a member of a cult or someone whose beliefs are cult-like, you are not wrestling with flesh and blood. You are facing a spirit of religious deception. Reason is meaningless, and intelligent debate is usually an exercise in futility. A close friend once told me, "You cannot argue with a demon." But you can pray, and you can persistently demonstrate the love of Christ. The anointing of the Spirit will break every yoke.

Materialism and Passivity

As devious and subtle as the doctrine of demons may be, an equally powerful deception is materialism—comfort in this life—and the spiritual passivity that accompanies it.

My father-in-law is the caretaker for several small avocado ranches in southern California. One sunny day, he was walking under the spreading branches of a large avocado tree when, heart pounding, he spied a mountain lion sprawled out on a limb immediately above him.

The big cat was sick, fortunately for him! He backed cautiously out of the shade, and a little later returned with another rancher and a high-powered rifle to put the animal out of its misery. But what a fright! Looking up and seeing a lion poised over your head! This is precisely the analogy the Bible uses to describe Satan: "Be self-controlled and alert. Your enemy the devil prowls around like a roaring lion looking for someone to devour" (1 Peter 5:8).

Now if you know anything about the habits of the lion, you know he much prefers to kill weak, unsuspecting victims. For all their fierce reputation, lions rely on their subtlety as much as their strength. In fact, I have heard that lions are basically lazy. Like a lion, Satan is looking for unsuspecting victims. If the forest were really teeming with lions and tigers and bears, you would never walk past the first tree. And if you had to, you would be sober and vigilant. This is why spiritual passivity is so perilous. It desensitizes us to the spiritual dimension.

The Bible teaches clearly the relationship between materialism and spiritual passivity. "Woe to you who are complacent in Zion," wrote Amos the prophet. "You lie on beds inlaid with ivory and lounge on your couches.

You dine on choice lambs and fattened calves. . . . Therefore you will be among the first to go into exile; your feasting and lounging will end" (Amos 6:1, 4, 7).

The prophecy of Jesus to the self-indulgent church in Laodicea was no less harsh:

> "You are lukewarm. . . . You say, 'I am rich; I have acquired wealth and do not need a thing.' But you do not realize that you are wretched, pitiful, poor, blind and naked. I counsel you to buy from me gold refined in the fire, so you can become rich [with the true riches] . . . and salve to put on your eyes, so you can see."   Revelation 3:16–18

Somehow, a life of ease and spiritual blindness always go hand in hand.

They are also a sign of the times. Revelation 18 describes the final collapse of Babylon, the consummate symbol of the world system and the pleasure of this age:

> "For all the nations have drunk the maddening wine of her [Babylon's] adulteries. The kings of the earth committed adultery with her, and the merchants of the earth grew rich from her excessive luxuries."
> verse 3

And more! It is here that we see how the world system, excessive materialism and spiritual blindness are directly linked to evil spirits: "Fallen! Fallen is Babylon the Great! She has become a home for demons" (verse 2). And what does God warn Christians? "Come out of her, my people, so that you will not share in her sins, so that you will not receive any of her plagues" (verse 4). As I said earlier, what feels good now may make you feel terrible later.

Nehemiah gives us a picture of failure and consequent captivity in his analysis of the ancient Jews:

> "Even while they were in their kingdom, enjoying your great goodness to them in the spacious and fertile land you gave them, they did not serve you or turn from their evil ways. But see, we are slaves today, slaves in the land you gave our forefathers. . . . Because of our sins, its abundant harvest goes to the kings you have placed over us. They rule over our bodies and our cattle as they please. We are in great distress."   Nehemiah 9:35–37

Doing your own thing, living your own life leads to spiritual blindness, and spiritual blindness leads to spiritual captivity.

To summarize, *the growing interest in spiritual matters is not a fad. It is a sign of the times. The Bible predicts that the last days will be characterized by an inundation of demonic power, evil and wickedness.* The abyss will be opened, and we will know it by the rise of multiple religions, new doctrines and spiritual deception. The basis for the deception will be pervasive spiritual passivity and blindness. But for us who are anchored to Jesus, "Thanks be to God, who always leads us in triumphal procession in Christ" (2 Corinthians 2:14).

3

The Clash of the Kingdoms

"The God of heaven will set up a kingdom that will
never be destroyed. . . . It will crush all those kingdoms and bring them to an end, but it will itself endure forever."   Daniel 2:44

The Bible records a bloody battleground. It pulls back the
curtain on the cosmic drama of two kingdoms played out
on the stage of human history. The story of the Bible opens
with the serpent's primeval challenge of God's newly created order, and it culminates with the ultimate triumph of
Jesus. Genesis describes how the struggle begins. Revelation reveals how the kingdoms of this world finally become the Kingdom of our God and of His Christ.

The rest of Scripture—its history, its story of redemption, its prophecy—is concerned with the struggle to establish that Kingdom. Until that final event unfolds, when
Jesus Christ will reign forever and ever, the saints of God
have a commission: to proclaim the Kingdom of God.

From the world's point of view, the Church is generally
irrelevant, but from God's perspective, the saints are the
light of the world and the salt of the earth. We are the key
players in this drama. God was incarnate in the Man

Christ Jesus, and now the Lord Jesus is present in the saints.* The Church is Christ present in the world. "[God's] intent was that now, through the church, the manifold wisdom of God should be made known to the rulers and authorities in the heavenly realms" (Ephesians 3:10).

In His final recorded prayer, Jesus established forever the destiny of every Christian: "As you sent me into the world, I have sent them into the world" (John 17:18). Thus, Satan's singular focus is to resist God's purpose by making war on the saints.

A Theology of the Kingdom

The term *Great Commission* is found nowhere in the New Testament, but it has been used to identify the command Jesus gave His disciples to go into all the world and preach the Gospel. Actually, the Great Commission is more than a call to missions in the traditional sense. It is a recommissioning to represent the authority of the King in every aspect of life.

The Commission was first given in Genesis 1. The creation of the human race was accompanied by God's declaration, "Let us make man in our image, in our likeness, *and let them rule*" (verse 26). The very first thing that God said about us was that we were created to rule, to have dominion, to be representatives of His Kingdom order in the earth. The terms *kingdom* and *dominion* are virtually interchangeable, because *kingdom* is derived from *king* and *dominion*. A kingdom is the dominion of a king. And Jesus is King where Jesus is Lord.

This Great Commission to have dominion is detailed in

---

* Jesus is present in the saints in the sense that the Church is His Body. Salvation is Christ in us. Salvation is not, however, deification.

verse 28: "God blessed them and said to them, 'Be fruitful and increase in number; fill the earth and subdue it. Rule over . . . every living creature that moves on the ground.' " One of these living things—"creeping things" as described in verse 26 (KJV)—was the serpent, Satan himself, suggesting that the Kingdom Commission was to include the spiritual realm.

The Commission is repeated in Psalm 8. After extolling the glories of God's magnificent universe, David asked the ageless question, "What is man?" (Psalm 8:4). Who are we? Why were we created? What purpose do we have in the vastness of the cosmos? The answer follows: "You have made him *to have dominion* over the works of Your hands" (verse 6, NKJV).

But in Genesis 3 it becomes clear to us that there is a fallen creature whose singular purpose is to prevent God from establishing His Kingdom order in the earth, and he does this by challenging man's right to represent the Creator. In the great conflict of Genesis 3, man failed to take dominion over the creeping serpent, and Satan successfully undermined the Kingdom Commission.

When man sinned, he not only lost his relationship with God, he lost his spiritual dominion as well. Instead of having dominion, man became dominated—by sin, by himself and by Satan. Instead of remaining representatives of God's Kingdom, human persons became subjects of the kingdom of darkness.

The Kingdom Theme through the Old Testament

The original purpose of God for humans as representatives of His Kingdom in the earth was thwarted in Eden, and the Old Testament presents a selective history of

God's attempt, through man, to reestablish His divine rule and order.

God began the process with the messianic promise to Adam and Eve immediately after their sin. Their offspring, Jesus, the seed of the woman, would one day crush the head of the serpent. The patriarchs (Abraham, Isaac, Jacob) headed that chosen lineage. Later, the principles of divine order—the Law—were given in detail through Moses. Later still, God appealed to His people to embrace His Kingdom order in the theocratic monarchies of Judah and Israel, but without success.

The dream of God's Kingdom on the earth was never fully realized in the Old Testament, but the Jewish nation was left with prophetic hope that the coming Messiah would ultimately reestablish the Kingdom of God on the earth. The Old Testament points forward to a golden age, prefigured in the kingdom of David and predicted again and again by the prophets.

A time would come when the mountain of the house of the Lord, the centerpiece and high place of Jewish worship, would be established above all the other mountains (Isaiah 2:2). Perhaps we could say there would be a kind of return to Eden: The lion would lie down with the lamb. God's order and law would prevail once again.

The Old Testament, then, begins with the conflict of the kingdoms. It ends with that conflict unresolved, but with the prophetic expectation that the kingdoms of this world will one day become the Kingdom of God and of His Christ.

Jesus and the Kingdom Commission

At this point the need for a Savior was clear, someone who could restore our broken relationship with the Father.

And along with that we needed someone who could crush the head of the serpent, who could restore man's dominion over God's ageless adversary, Satan. Jesus, of course, was that fulfillment. He came not only as Savior, but to rule as Lord, One who has dominion. Jesus came to resurrect the Kingdom Commission: "Have dominion . . . upon the earth" (Genesis 1:28, KJV).

According to the New Testament, Jesus of Nazareth fulfilled the prophecies of the Old Testament. He came to sit on the throne of David and establish God's Kingdom in the earth, albeit a different kind of kingdom than the popular Jewish notion of a political empire. Jesus declared that His Kingdom is not of this world and yet, paradoxically, we witness a very real and present manifestation of it. Jesus taught His disciples to pray like this: "Your kingdom come, your will be done *on earth* as it is in heaven" (Matthew 6:10).

Regardless of how much we may spiritualize the Kingdom, both the Church and her adversaries in the world— from early Romans to present-day Communists—have recognized that the coming spiritual Kingdom has a dramatic influence on the here and now. Christ's claim to a *spiritual* Kingdom did not assuage His adversaries. He was not a real political threat, and yet He was more of a menace to both Jews and Romans of His day than any aspiring politician or military leader could ever have hoped to be.

The Kingdom of heaven is God's rule and order entering a chaotic world. The work of the Son of God, according to John 1:1–5, is prefigured in the creation account: Jesus is light in the darkness, order in the chaos (see Genesis 1:1–5). For the New Testament writers Matthew and Luke, this Kingdom of God in Christ meant two things: a new way of living, and an outpouring of divine power to validate that lifestyle and to overcome the powers that resist it. Everything that Jesus "began to do and to teach" (Acts 1:1) is somehow related to the Kingdom. He taught the principles of the Kingdom with Kingdom authority, and He did the works of the Kingdom with Kingdom power.

"From that time on [from the time of His baptism in water and in the Spirit] Jesus began to preach, 'Repent, for the kingdom of heaven is near' " (Matthew 4:17). This little summary of the ministry of Christ sets the stage for the Sermon on the Mount in Matthew 5–7, which represents the greatest single collection of the teachings of Christ. Its theme? Principles of the Kingdom! Strikingly, the Beatitudes, which introduce the Sermon, open and close with references to Kingdom lifestyle.

Jesus taught with authority (Matthew 7:29), not like the scribes and the Pharisees whose authority was based on intellect and tradition, but with the real power of God demonstrated by His works: "Jesus went throughout Galilee, teaching . . . [and] preaching the good news of the kingdom, and healing every disease and sickness among the people" (Matthew 4:23).

So with a new twist, the New Testament claims that Jesus is King, fulfilling the messianic promises of the Old Testament. He is the One who has bruised the head of the serpent. As John wrote, "The reason the Son of God appeared was to destroy the devil's work" (1 John 3:8). Since the beginning of time, there has been a conflict of the kingdoms, and Christ is the Victor, the Conqueror—the King! God's Kingdom has come and will come. It has prevailed and will prevail. God's Kingdom will not be *fully* restored until Jesus comes again, but in the meantime, the saints have a commission to fulfill and a battle to win.

The Great Recommission

The Old Testament, then, is the story of the Kingdom—commission, abortion and prophetic expectation. The New Testament is the story of the Kingdom at hand. Jesus the Messiah came to fulfill the Old Testament prophetic hope and initiate the restoration of the Kingdom. He preached and demonstrated the Kingdom of God in His earthly ministry, and He crushed the head of the serpent in His death and resurrection. In so doing He destroyed the power base of the kingdom of darkness and made it possible once again for God's people to fulfill the Genesis commission to have dominion.

This is clear in the final chapter of Matthew: "All authority in heaven and on earth [absolute dominion] has been given to me" (28:18). Why do we bypass this verse? Why are we so ignorant of the conflict of the kingdoms underlying this declaration? This is the hinge of Bible history. What God has done in Christ is being transferred to God's people in a Great *Re*commission. What the saints in the Old Testament had only dreamed of is about to occur. "Therefore [because of the reestablishment of God's authority in the earth through Christ] go and make disciples of all nations" (Matthew 28:18–19)

We must realize that the Great Commission is directly related to spiritual warfare. And that the fulfillment of the Great Commission requires an understanding of the clash of the kingdoms and the dynamics of spiritual conflict. Unfortunately, Satan understands the purposes of God far better than the saints understand the plans of hell.

Jesus promised that the gates, or counsels, of hell will not prevail against the Church, but this assumes that we are not ignorant of those counsels. The Bible is a battle manual, and one of its basic premises is that we wrestle not against flesh and blood. Our spiritual enemies are very real. The Kingdom of God cannot be established in anyone's life, let alone in the world, without a direct confrontation with the unholy one.

Kingdom Conflict Today

Perhaps one of the greatest mysteries of the Bible is that Jesus is Lord, and yet in the present moment we do not actually see all things in subjection to Him (Hebrews 2:8). Jesus won the battle. "It is finished," Jesus proclaimed on the cross. The work of redemption is over. Never again will there be another sacrifice. Never again will there be another door of salvation. God has spoken with finality through the mouth of His Son (Hebrews 1:1–2). We refer to this as the positional or legal aspect of salvation. The will is signed.

And yet the work of the Kingdom and the battle to spread its influence continues. Much of the will remains to be executed. Satan still has influence in the world, just as "the old man" still has influence in the life of the believer. We must resist the devil and put off the old man. There is a mountain of literature on Christian growth and discipleship, but what about spiritual warfare? D. Martyn Lloyd-Jones wrote in *The Christian Warfare* not too many years ago,

> It has been a very striking fact concerning Christian life and witness since about 1880—and I am referring particularly to evangelical Christian life—that very little of this kind of literature [on spiritual warfare] has been produced. . . . No one seemed to be concerned about this

conflict against the "principalities and powers," about how to stand against "the wiles of the devil" (p. 149).

How can we recognize our spiritual enemies? And more, how can we resist and overcome them? What are Satan's devices?

Satan's plan is complex and uniquely designed for each situation. In other words, the devil has a plan for your life. Satan's strategies fall into three general categories or strongholds. We will identify and define each of these in a moment, but first allow me to give you a little background on the common biblical idea of mountains, strongholds and high places.

Mountain in the Bible is frequently a figure of speech for Kingdom authority. This is derived from the fact that the ancient nations had private gods, each of whom was honored in a geographical high place. One of Israel's kings, for example, Hezekiah, is reported to have "removed the high places," the hilltop sites of pagan worship that dotted Israel during its days of spiritual decline (2 Kings 18:3–4).

Why was this necessary? Because the power of pagan kingdoms was believed to reside in the authority of the local gods. The high place, or stronghold, was the spiritual control center of the nation that worshiped the gods who lived there. This is why the Philistine capture of the Ark of the Covenant in 1 Samuel 4 was so significant. To capture the god of another nation, they believed, rendered that nation powerless. To have their god was to have their power. From the perspective of the New Testament, the pagan "gods" were demon principalities and powers.

This helps us understand what Jesus meant when He declared, "If you have faith as a grain of mustard seed, you can move *mountains.*" *Mountain* is a biblical symbol, not merely of the greatest obstacles of life, but beyond, of the spiritual forces behind those barriers. Paul undoubtedly had this in mind when he wrote to the Corinthians, "The weapons we fight with are not the weapons of the world. On the contrary, they have divine power to demolish *strongholds*" (2 Corinthians 10:4).

Satan's Strongholds Today

These strongholds, then, fall into three broad categories: territorial, ideological and personal.

One: Territorial Strongholds

These have to do with the hierarchy of dark beings that are strategically assigned by Satan himself to influence and control nations, communities and even families. A multilevel system of spiritual beings is suggested by Ephesians 6:12: rulers, authorities, the powers of this dark world, the spiritual forces of evil.

C. Peter Wagner, author of numerous books on the principles of church growth, has been researching the subject of spiritual warfare and territorial spirits for several years. He has concluded that identifying and pulling down the strongholds of territorial spirits is one of the most significant factors in church growth or the success of ministry. Wagner's hypothesis, offered at the Academic Symposium on Power Evangelism at Fuller Seminary, is

> that Satan delegates high-ranking members of the hierarchy of evil spirits to control nations, regions, cities, tribes, people groups, neighborhoods, and other significant social networks of human beings throughout the

world. Their major assignment is to prevent God from being glorified in their territory which they do through directing the activity of lower-ranking demons.

In the Old Testament, the angel Gabriel apparently wrestled with a territorial spirit: "I have come in response to [your prayers, Daniel]. But the prince of the Persian kingdom resisted me twenty-one days. Then Michael, one of the chief princes, came to help me, because I was detained there with the king of Persia" (Daniel 10:12–13).

There is a growing awareness in the Church of the power of territorial spirits. Recently, I met Dr. Paul Cho, pastor in Seoul, South Korea, of the largest church in the history of Christianity. Speaking to a ministers' luncheon on the subject of prayer, he told the story of an American chaplain stationed in Korea who was having an unusually good response to his ministry among U.S. military personnel.

He visited Dr. Cho and asked him, "Why am I so much more effective in Korea than I was in Europe? Same minister, same message, same kind of audience—American servicemen—but significantly different results." Dr. Cho's answer: The spiritual "air" is clearer over Korea, because tens of thousands of Korean Christians are praying fervently.

Have you ever attended a church camp or retreat away from a metropolitan area? Why do you suppose it "feels" better in the mountains or in the forest? Why do you think it is so much easier to seek God? Certainly the social environment of Christian camping has its effects, but I believe the spiritual highs we experience in those settings are due largely to the general absence of principalities and powers in the air.

The missions director on our church staff attended the

great Lausanne conference on world evangelism in Manila
in the summer of 1989. She reported that "territorial spirits" was a subject of great interest and inquiry. One of the
most striking examples of the influence of territorial
strongholds, and the power of Christ to break those
strongholds, was reported by Edgardo Silvoso in "Spiritual Warfare in Argentina and the 'Plan Resistencia' (the
Plan of Resistance)," a workshop at the conference. I have
excerpted portions of the report:

> The Argentine Church never experienced great growth.
> The average congregation was smaller than 100 members.
>
> Then in 1983 something happened that changed all that.
> Carlos Annacondia, a lay preacher, was invited to hold a
> crusade [in a church in La Plata]. After four months of
> boldly preaching the Word and heavily relying on spiritual
> warfare, over 40,000 had made public commitments to
> Christ. It was totally unheard of.
>
> As the churches grew in their understanding of spiritual
> warfare, one aspect that became clear was that of territorial
> powers.
>
> In the fall of 1984 a group of pastors and leaders gathered
> [to pray for] 109 towns within 100 miles [that] had no Chris-
> tian witness.
>
> The pastors and leaders came together in one accord and
> placed the entire area under spiritual authority. Positioning
> themselves across the street from the headquarters of Mr.
> Meregildo's [a warlock famous for his dramatic cures] fol-
> lowers they served an eviction notice on the forces of evil.
>
> Less than three years later 82 of those towns had evan-
> gelical churches in them.

Second: Ideological Strongholds

These have to do with world views and the correspond-
ing lifestyles that are contrary to God's Word. These are

ideas, philosophies and religious or nonreligious views that influence culture and society. Examples are political ideologies, like socialism or Communism; philosophical ideologies, like secular humanism or evolutionary materialism; and religious ideologies, like Unitarianism, Islam or New Age thinking.

These views may or may not be carefully defined, but they are ways of thinking that have a powerful and profound effect on society, and thus on individuals. The New Age, for example, has no commonly accepted doctrinal statement. It is not a conspiracy, as such, but there are certain aspects of the movement that are generally identifiable and that greatly influence the way people think and live.

Hollywood has not written a plot for the takeover of the American mind, yet every time you turn on your television you are risking the influence of whatever ideology lies beneath the surface of the program you watch. Our colleges and universities are cauldrons of persuasive ideologies. "See to it," Paul warns, "that no one takes you captive through hollow and deceptive philosophy, which depends on human tradition and the basic principles of this world rather than on Christ" (Colossians 2:8).

It is true that not all of these ideologies are specifically demonic in origin, but all of them do have roots in Satan's master plan. They are what Paul calls "arguments and every pretension that sets itself up against the knowledge of God" (2 Corinthians 10:5). The important factor here is that we are dealing not merely with human ideas, but with human ideas that have an essential spiritual power. If we recognize their source, our resistance to these ideologies must be spiritual, not merely intellectual.

Third: Personal Strongholds

These have to do with you—your thoughts, your feelings, your attitudes, your behavior patterns. Paul writes in 2 Corinthians 10:3, "For though we live in the world, we do not wage war as the world does." Life is full of spiritual influences, and spiritual power can be countered only with spiritual power.

Thus, "the weapons we fight with are not the weapons of the world. On the contrary, they have divine power to demolish strongholds. . . . We take captive every thought to make it obedient to Christ" (verses 4–5). Your mind, your thought life is a battleground, not just between the old you and the new you, but with outside spiritual influences as well. We will be examining personal strongholds in great detail in our chapters on the armor of God next, in the second section of this book.

Resisting and overcoming the devil begins with a recognition of the reality of the battle. Furthermore, success in spiritual warfare is grounded in a clear understanding of the wiles of the devil. My prayer, with Paul, is that "Satan might not outwit us. For we are not unaware of his schemes" (2 Corinthians 2:11).

Part Two
The Armor of God
Resisting the Dominion of Darkness

4
Resisting the Devil

Resist the devil, and he will flee from you.
James 4:7

Life is a spiritual battle. "Our struggle is not against flesh and blood, but . . . against the powers of this dark world and against the spiritual forces of evil in the heavenly realms" (Ephesians 6:12).

If this is true, and we have seen that it is, then the development of our spiritual sensitivity and power is absolutely necessary. Unfortunately, there is only one way for this to happen: experience. The troubles of life are actually opportunities to build up your faith and strengthen your relationship with God. They make you a more skilled and effective soldier of the Kingdom.

Faith comes by hearing the Word of God (Romans 10:17), but faith does not grow without exercise. Reading the Bible without practicing its principles in the arena of life is like reading tennis magazines without ever walking onto a court. All the training videos in the world will never make you a tennis player. Reading about war does not make you a soldier, but basic training and combat will!

Romans 5:3–4 unfolds the process of spiritual development: "We . . . rejoice in our sufferings." Why? "Because we know that suffering produces perseverance; perseverance [produces] character; and character [produces] hope."

The apostle Paul almost seemed to welcome trouble, not because trouble is pleasant, but because it gave him an opportunity to grow in his faith.

James had the same unusual way of looking at life: "Consider it pure joy, my brothers, whenever you face trials of many kinds." Why? "Because you know that the testing of your faith develops perseverance" (James 1:2–3).

Resistance Means You Will Get Stronger

Bodybuilding is based on the principle of resistance: the more weight, the more the resistance; and the more the resistance, the more the muscles develop. Competition weight lifters welcome resistance. In fact, they keep increasing it to push their strength to the limit. Respect Satan's power, but don't fear it. Accept it as a challenge to practice your faith.

Spiritual resistance is spiritual bodybuilding. It increases the strength of your faith, and faith-building, like exercise, I'm sorry to say, is impossible without effort.

This year my wife and I returned to Kansas for our college reunion. We had not been on the campus for twenty years, but the memories were as fresh as the sunrise that morning.

After walking around the campus, I wanted to spend a few final moments standing on the soccer field where I practiced and played for two years. Do you know what I remembered the most? The agony of the first week of practice and the painful walk from the showers to the cafeteria for the evening meal.

Exercise does not create new muscles; it lets you discover and strengthen the ones you have. Trouble in life does not give you faith. Only Jesus can do that. But life's battles have the potential of increasing your spiritual strength, provided you use them to exercise your faith. With every problem there is a solution. With every temptation, God will provide a way of escape. You can either think of life as full of problems or full of opportunities.

The author of Hebrews saw value in the exercise and pain of life when he wrote, "No discipline seems pleasant at the time, but painful. Later on, however, it produces a harvest of righteousness and peace for those who have been trained [exercised] by it" (Hebrews 12:11). The weights of life will either crush you or exercise you. The devil will either destroy you or act as an opponent to test your spiritual skills. If you give in to the pain and give up, he will devour you. Resist him and he will flee from you.

Resistance Means "to Stand Against"

Resistance means "to stand against," as in a resistance movement. Freedom-fighters refuse to say *die* in the face of insurmountable odds, even if death is certain. The Greek term translated "resist" in James 4:7 and 1 Peter 5:9, where we are told to resist the devil, is *anthistemi* (or *antihistemi*), which means literally "to stand against." Obviously, it is the term from which we derive our English word *antihistamine*. An antihistamine is medication that helps you "stand against" the symptoms of sinus allergies or the common cold.

The armor of God, described in Ephesians 6, and which we will study in the next few chapters, is our best means of resistance. In fact, resistance to spiritual darkness is high when you are wearing the whole armor of God, and it is impossible "to stand against" the devil when you are not.

Round-the-clock resistance to the devil, however, is not

normally necessary. "Therefore put on the full armor of God, so that *when the day of evil comes*, you may be able to stand your ground" (Ephesians 6:13). Not every day is evil. Not every problem is from the devil. This is further suggested by the tense of the Greek word *resist* in both James 4:7 and 1 Peter 5:9. What we have here in the Greek text is an aoristic action, an occurrence as opposed to something continuous and ongoing.

If there is a danger in spiritual warfare, it is giving the devil too much attention. Resisting the devil in your personal life is necessary only when he comes against you. Pray constantly and practice the presence of God, but do not get into the trap of practicing the presence of Satan by seeing demons in every doorknob. Again, it is like lifting weights. You cannot do it 24 hours a day. Too much exercise will kill you.*

Resisting the Devil and Restraining Yourself

Another word for "resist" is *restrain*, and a synonym of "restrain" is *bind*. When you resist the devil you restrain him, and when you restrain him you bind him. You bind the devil with your actions, not just your words. He is powerless when you resist him, because he is bound by your resistance.

Resisting the devil, then, begins with restraining yourself. Self-control is taught in 1 Peter 5:5–9 as preliminary to

*An exception may be when a person is committed to intercession and prayer against a particular spiritual stronghold or territorial spirit. Some people have called this "storming the gates of hell," an aggressive attack against a particular principality. I address this in chapter 12.

spiritual warfare. In other words, you cannot rule the devil effectively if you cannot rule yourself.

Hapuna Beach is one of the largest and most popular strands of sand on the Kona Coast of Hawaii's Big Island. A large sign confronts you as you walk toward the ocean: "Warning. Dangerous currents. If you get caught in the current, *don't panic*. Let the current carry you out to sea. It will weaken, and you will be able to swim back to shore."

Life is full of currents that carry us places we really don't want to go. Most are circumstantial. Some are spiritual. Often it is not possible to overcome the current immediately, and the most effective resistance is just keeping our composure. Self-control alone can garner great spiritual victories.

The opposite of self-control is panic. I was once within a few breaths of drowning. Snorkeling is really a very safe and simple sport. Elderly people do it. Children do it. But one time my friend Tim wanted us to swim a fair distance into the open ocean, beyond the shelter of a rocky cove. He also convinced me that I could not really enjoy myself unless I wore a weight belt to make me less buoyant in the event I decided to dive.

It was more than I was prepared to handle. Deep water. Ocean swells. A leaky face mask. And the weight belt helping my sinking body along. I started gulping for air as panic set in, the prelude to drowning. My only hope was to cling to a jagged rock, made even more dangerous by an encrustation of barnacles and sea urchins.

I decided in a flash to trade oblivion in the blue Pacific for a painful climb on the rocks. My friend screamed at me, "Don't do it!" But I had no choice. I knew I had to regain my composure. I did, and I am alive to tell the story, albeit with the memory of bleeding shins stained purple by sea urchin spines.

Winning life's battles often requires a cool head. And if you want the upper hand over the dominion of darkness, be sober and vigilant. Be watchful and alert. Resist the devil by restraining yourself. Paul suggests this when he writes, "Don't let the sun go down on your anger." In other words, don't let your emotions get the best of you. "And do not give the devil a foothold" (Ephesians 4:26–27).

Resisting the Devil, Not People

There is a fine line between resisting the devil, who frequently works through other people, and resisting the people who are his unwitting instruments. In Matthew 5:39 Jesus cautions us, "Do not resist [*anti-histemi*] an evil person."

When I first discovered this reference in the context of my study of *resist,* it puzzled me. Then I realized that Jesus is simply telling us, "Don't stand up for yourself all the time. Let God fight your battles. God alone is your defense against the devil and the people he influences for evil."

Sometimes resistance means "going with the flow" without losing an ounce of faith that God is ultimately going to win the battle for you. Resisting and resting seem contradictory, but resisting the devil and resting in God go hand in hand. Sometimes the best resistance is no resistance.

Jesus is our example: "Christ suffered for you, leaving you an example, that you should follow in his steps. 'He committed no sin, and no deceit was found in his mouth.' When they hurled their insults at him, he did not retaliate. [He restrained Himself, but He did not cave in to the pressure.] . . . Instead [and this is the key], he entrusted himself to him who judges justly" (1 Peter 2:21–23). The

Kingdom must be taken by force, but the force is the cross—renouncing self-trust and clinging to God. Resist the devil, but be kind to people, even if they are your enemies (Matthew 5:44).*

Putting on the Armor

Spiritual warfare is a difficult and demanding business. Our adversary is the second-most powerful being in the universe. He is highly intelligent, clever beyond measure and cannot be outwitted. The only effective spiritual antihistamine, then, is the armor of God.

"Finally, be strong in the Lord and in his mighty power. Put on the armor of God so that you can take your stand against the devil's schemes" (Ephesians 6:10–11). The armor of God is "his mighty power."

Only by the power of God and our authority in Jesus are we able to resist and overcome the dominion of darkness. The mountains of life and the strongholds of our spiritual enemies are removed " 'not by [human] might nor by [human] power, but by my Spirit,' says the Lord Almighty" (Zechariah 4:6).

The Greek term translated "schemes" (Ephesians 6:11) is *methodeia* and means to follow a settled plan, to deceive, to use trickery. The mastery of Satan is in his elusiveness and cunning. He is the consummate magician, the master of subliminal messages. His work is always on the boundary of reality.

---

* Kindness is virtue, but we must always be careful to distinguish between genuine kindness and manipulative kindness, genuine love and manipulative love. Manipulative love is loving to get. I discuss this further in the last section of chapter 7.

Even a book like this on strategies for spiritual warfare is not adequate to uncover all of the devil's clever deceptions. In fact, Satan is so astute that a single, fail-safe plan against him is not even presented in the Bible. We are warned. We are told to submit to God. We are commanded to be sober and self-controlled and vigilant, and to resist the devil. But the subtleties of Satan's schemes can be uncovered only through prayer and careful discernment—and resisted by putting on the *full* armor of God.

Few of us, for example, would think of marriage and family as a habitation of demons. Warfare maybe, but not *spiritual* warfare. No husband or wife or angry teen would normally stop to consider the spiritual implications of a family argument, especially when he or she feels so offended, or so right.

Yet this is the deception. Paul's instruction about wrestling with spiritual darkness in Ephesians 6:10 concludes with *finally*, which takes us back to the paragraphs immediately preceding his passage on the armor of God. Many of you who are reading this now, and who are very familiar with the armor of God, might have difficulty recalling what leads up to Paul's discussion of spiritual warfare.

Look and see. His topics include "wives and husbands" (5:22–33), "parents and children" (6:1–4) and "slaves and masters," or to put it into terms we understand, "employers and employees" (6:5–9). After introducing these subjects, he concludes, "Finally, be strong in the Lord and in his mighty power" (6:10). In other words, if I understand Paul's logic, the armor of God and the principles of spiritual warfare are not limited in their application to exorcisms, occult practices and bizarre phenomena on exotic mission fields. We cannot disconnect spiritual warfare from the ordinary events of daily life.

The Full Armor of God: The Whole Church

All of the devil's schemes demand that we put on the *full* armor of God, not just one or two pieces. Overcoming the whole counsel of hell requires the whole counsel of God, which brings us to another crucial point. No one person has the whole counsel of God, especially in the broader aspects of spiritual warfare.

Rarely will spiritual warfare bring you face-to-face alone with the devil. Even overcoming personal temptations, which we label addictions today, often requires the support of other caring and praying people. Spiritual warfare is an activity of the whole Body of Christ working together. Jesus promised that the gates, or counsels, of hell would not prevail against *the Church.*

Tragically, few Christians, especially in North America where we pride ourselves in our individuality, understand our relationship to the whole. Every member of the Body of Christ has a gift and a function; any member detached from his place in the Body is powerless, even lifeless. In fact, there are probably few things more ghastly than a dismembered human body. Perhaps the Lord Jesus feels the same about His Body when the members fight among themselves and everyone does what is right in his own eyes.

The Greek of the New Testament, like many other languages, distinguishes between the singular and plural forms of *you*, both in the pronouns and in the endings of the verbs. Few English readers realize that nearly every *you* in the entire New Testament is actually plural. Using the phrase *you together* is probably a more accurate way to translate the plural Greek *you*, which dramatically discloses the emphasis of Ephesians 6:10–18. Look at verse 13 in this light:

Therefore *you together* put on the full armor of God
[help each other get dressed for battle], so that when
the day of evil comes, *you together* may be able to
stand your ground, and after *you together* have done
everything, to stand.

Spiritual warfare is Body ministry. A house divided
against itself cannot stand, but when there is spiritual
agreement, the power of God's people multiplies expo-
nentially. "You will pursue your enemies, and they will
fall by the sword before you. Five of you will chase a
hundred, and a hundred of you will chase ten thousand,
and your enemies will fall by the sword before you" (Le-
viticus 26:7–8).

So resist the powers of darkness by putting on the full
armor of God. Do it now. Do it together, beginning with
the belt of truth.

5
The Belt of Truth

Stand firm then, with the belt of truth buckled around
your waist.   Ephesians 6:14

Our youngest son, Matthew, had just finished kinder-
garten. One of the members of our congregation made
him a wooden chair, shaped and painted black and
white like a holstein cow. One day, my wife discovered
this little masterpiece of country folk art broken into two
pieces.

So we interrogated Matt to find out just how this happened. "My friend Amy. She broke it," he replied confidently. "I was just standing there."

I persisted with the cross-examination: "Did you have
anything to do with this at all?" Matt looked up at me with
his best innocent face: "No, Dad, *really!*"

But something deep in my heart said to me, *This kid is
not telling me the whole story.* So I warned him, "Next time
Amy comes over to play, I'm going to ask her what really
happened."

I knew full well that Matt would not like this proposal.
Amy is a couple of years older and has more savvy—*and* a
better memory, I suspected.

"If you are not telling me the whole story, Matt, if Amy

tells me something different, you'll get a spanking. But I won't punish you if you tell me the truth now."

He studied me for a moment and, without saying another word, hopped away into another room. I was disappointed. My strategy had failed. Strange, isn't it, how a five-year-old can be so controlling!

But after about fifteen minutes, he came back into the front room and sat quietly on the sofa. I watched him over the top of my newspaper as he stared up at the wall. I knew what was going through his little mind, and I was supremely delighted. He was about to tell the truth! I reopened the conversation: "Do you want to tell me what really happened now?"

"Yes," he answered. With surprising objectivity for a five-year-old, he recounted the incident. He had stood on the cow, he reported, grabbed it by the head, and given it a few brutal shakes. Amy had done the same thing, and the unfortunate wooden animal had collapsed on the bedroom floor.

"Matt!" I exclaimed. "I am so happy you told me the truth!" And I was. Telling the truth was far more important than whether or not he broke one of his toys. Kids will be kids. Kids will make mistakes—but truthfulness is forever. To put it in biblical terms, Matt was putting on the belt of truth.

"Stand firm then, with the belt of truth buckled around your waist." The belt of truth is the first of the six elements of armor in Ephesians 6. What is the belt of truth? Perhaps we should begin by talking about what it is not. The belt of truth, in this context, is *not* merely correct creed or doctrinal orthodoxy.

Nor is the belt of truth the same as the sword of the Spirit, something Paul addresses a few verses later. As we will see, the sword of the Spirit is an *offensive* weapon. It is the confession of our mouths. The sword of the Spirit is the power of God's Word. The belt of truth, on the other hand, refers to the condition of your private life, truth inside of you—truth guarding your private parts, so to speak. The King James translation is vivid: "Gird up your loins with truth."

The classic commentary *Expositor's Greek Testament* defines the belt of truth as "the personal grace of *candor, sincerity, truthfulness.* . . . [And] the mind that will practice no deceits and attempt no disguises . . . is indeed vital to Christian safety" (Vol. III, p. 386).

The aggressiveness of your public confession ("the sword of the Word") can never substitute for personal integrity ("the belt of truthfulness") and an inner life that relates properly to God. In marriage, for example, David and Karen Mains call this "mental fidelity." People see your outward behaviors, but God sees into your heart. No doubt this is why the first step in preparation for spiritual battle is to put on the belt of truth, in order to ensure that everything in your private life, as far as you know, is right with God.

You cannot even begin to think of standing up in spiritual warfare unless you are first committed to personal integrity. Congregational confession and public ministry are meaningless without the belt of truth "girding up your loins." On the other hand, the collapse of ministry, the destruction of your life and home, begins when you allow the tempter entrance into your heart. And this happens, literally, when you compromise your conscience and settle for anything less than the truth.

The national religious scandals of the '80s began just like this, with failure to put on the belt of truth and the violation of personal convictions. Like Ananias and Sapphira (Act 5:1 *ff.*), you may be lying to yourself, to others and even to God—and be completely unaware that Satan has filled your heart. The belt of truth is not the facts you believe about the Bible. It's your way of life.

Telling Yourself the Truth

The ancient introduction to Psalm 51 puts it in the context of a real-life situation: "For the director of music. A psalm of David. When the prophet Nathan came to him after David had committed adultery with Bathsheba." Psalm 51 is about private sin, painstakingly covered by David and painfully exposed by the prophet Nathan.

"Have mercy on me, O God, according to your unfailing love," David wept in anguish. "According to your great compassion blot out my transgressions. Wash away all my iniquity and cleanse me from my sin. . . . Against you, you only, have I sinned" (verses 1–4). And in verse 6 David concedes, "Surely you desire truth *in the inner parts.*" God does not just have His eye on my public behavior. He wants to shine the light of His Word into every crevice and corner of my mind. If He doesn't, I will not be prepared to resist and overcome my spiritual enemies.

What is the belt of truth? Having a pure heart before God, and its corollary, being honest with yourself. The opposite of self-honesty is self-deception. Psychologists call this denial. Denial, for example, is a root of alcoholism. Alcohol is a substitute. It puts the mind to sleep. A heavy drinker does not have to think about his problems or face reality. Most importantly, he does not have to face himself.

For someone who has a problem with alcohol, alcohol is not the problem. The person is the problem, and the solution to the problem is being willing to face oneself. Denial is avoidance of that problem. But denial is not the exclusive domain of alcoholics. Denial is at the root of all human sin.

What happened when King David fell into sin? He lusted for a beautiful woman and forced himself on her. It did not seem to matter to him that he was taking another man's wife. The raging river of lust was so powerful that the consequences of sin were, for the moment, inconsequential. Besides, David was king. He could do anything he wanted.

But Bathsheba became pregnant. Now David felt guilty, not because he had sinned, but because he might get caught. Instead of confessing his evil to God and cleaning up his life, he schemed to exonerate himself. He manipulated people and circumstances so that he would not have to face himself and deal with his sin.

Bathsheba's husband, Uriah, was on active military duty. So David recalled him from the front lines of battle for some "r and r." David expected Uriah to have an evening or two with his wife. Her pregnancy, then, could be easily explained. Uriah was delighted to come home, but slept on the front step of David's palace and refused time alone with his wife. How could he enjoy himself, he reasoned, when his comrades were sacrificing themselves on the field of battle?

One lie led to another. Frustrated, David devised an even more dastardly plan. He prepared written orders to send Uriah into the battle and to abandon him in the thick of the fight, ensuring his death. And worse, he had Uriah deliver the sealed document—his own death certificate—personally!

What a great way to solve his problem, David presumed. Now he could marry this woman legitimately, and no one would discover his sin. But Nathan cleverly exposed his king's treachery. He told David a heartrending story about a little pet lamb, confiscated from a poor family by an evil rich man. At first David wanted to throw the man into prison. But when he realized he himself was the culprit in the parable, David's anger over the purported injustice turned to wrenching sorrow and repentance. (See Psalm 32.)

David's initial denial is utterly irrational, but you know as well as I that every one of us has reacted the same way. "Who broke the toy, Matt?" "Amy broke it." Our lying, our deception, our manipulation of others can be so clever we surprise ourselves! Think about where you work. It may even be in a church! Are people around you always truthful? Are they honest with others? Are they honest with themselves?

We live in a society where lying and denial, double-talk and misinformation are commonplace. In an American presidential election, the most popular and important decision of our democratic process, few of us really know what to believe or who is telling the truth.

The problem of denial and self-deception is basic to virtually all of life's problems. Have you, for example, had your spouse or friend become unexpectedly testy about something? And when you pressed him, he made it clear he did not want to discuss it? Or worse, he gave you some half-truth, or maybe even made you feel guilty for asking?

What we are facing here is not merely a human problem. Satan is the great liar, and hell itself is the fountainhead of all deceit. In *People of the Lie*, psychiatrist Scott Peck* writes,

> As well as being the Father of Lies, Satan may be said to be a spirit of mental illness. In *The Road Less Traveled* I defined mental health as "an ongoing process of dedication to reality at all costs." Satan is utterly dedicated to opposing that process. In fact, the best definition I have for Satan is that it is *a real spirit of unreality*. The paradoxical reality of this spirit must be recognized (p. 207).

Why do we lie? Why are we so easily self-deceived? We do it to protect ourselves, we think, and yet the very thing we do to save our skins is what destroys us. "The man who loves his life will lose it, while the man who hates his life in this world will keep it"(John 12:25). To have a pure heart before God means that you are honest with yourself. To put on the belt of truth means that you must first renounce the cover-up of denial. Denial is false armor; self-honesty is risky. It feels as if you are undressing in public! But self-honesty actually brings God into your life, and you cannot ask for better protection than that.

The story of David is only one of many in the Bible about people who would not face their sins, who would not face themselves. When Adam and Eve sinned, God could not find them. "Why are you hiding?" He asked. "And those fig leaves? Why are you trying to protect your-

* Peck has been referred to by some as a Christian psychiatrist. Much of his work, however, is unorthodox. Peck should be read with caution. Howard Pepper in "The Works of M. Scott Peck—A Summary Critique" (*Christian Research Journal*, Winter/Spring 1988, pp. 28–30) writes, "There is much to learn from Peck and there is much to beware."

selves? Who told you that you were naked?" What we read in Genesis 3:8–13 is the first recorded human conversation with God after the Fall. Adam spoke first: "The woman [denial] whom *You* gave me [more denial], she made me eat." Then Eve: "The devil made me do it [still more denial]."

Genesis 4 tells the story of Cain and Abel. Cain's offering of grain was not acceptable to God, which made him very angry about the apparent injustice of God's favor on his brother, Abel. Surprisingly, God never really told him *why* his offering was unacceptable, but He warned Cain that his response was crucial. Sin was lurking at his door, waiting to consume him.

We cannot always guarantee God's response to our "offerings," but regardless of what happens, regardless of what we *think* should happen, we are always responsible for our reactions. I am never accountable for what God does or does not do. I am always accountable for me.

Cain refused to take responsibility for his attitudes and behavior, went out into the field and killed his brother. "Where is Abel?" God inquired of Cain. "I don't know. Am I my brother's keeper?" Cain was unwilling to be honest with himself.

And then there was Aaron's peculiar behavior at Sinai told in Exodus 32. God was giving the Law to Moses, and it was taking an interminably long time. The Israelites did not even know if Moses was still alive, and no one dared ascend the mountain to look for him, what with all of that lightning and thunder. So they insisted on creating their own god. Aaron buckled easily under their demand and fashioned a golden calf.

As Moses returned from the mountain, he was puzzled by all the commotion in the camp. When he saw the Israelites worshiping the golden image, he smashed the tablets of stone, symbolizing the broken covenant. In anger and disbelief he demanded an explanation. Aaron's response was audacious denial: "Do not be angry, my lord. You know how prone *these people* are to evil." Unbelievable! Aaron was the ringleader! And then this: "So I told them, 'Whoever has any gold jewelry, take it off.' Then they gave me the gold, and I threw it into the fire, *and out came this calf!*" (verse 24).

We laugh at Aaron's ridiculous excuse. It reminds us of something our kids would say when they get caught with their hands in the cookie jar. But it's really not funny. Denial is the terrible root of all human sin: Adam and Eve bringing sin into the human race. Cain killing his brother. Aaron and the Israelites worshiping an idol. David committing adultery and murder. It is no different today.

The Consequences of Denial

At least three things happen when we indulge in persistent denial.

First, we are alienated from God. We cannot stand before His righteousness. Look at Adam and Eve hiding in the Garden.

Second, we are alienated from one another. Look at Cain's murderous anger.

I just read in the newspaper that a man in a rage ran over three people with his truck, all because of an argument over who would bring home the beer. Denial destroys relationships. Sometimes it even destroys other people because the one who denies his own sin must blame someone else. "Scapegoating" is what we call it. "The woman, she made me eat the forbidden fruit."

Third, we self-destruct. David confessed, "When I re-mained silent and refused to confess my sins, when I would not face myself, my bones wasted away and my strength was sapped as in the heat of summer" (Psalm 32:3–4, my paraphrase). God forgave him, but David's kingdom was never the same after his little fling with adultery.

God is incredibly patient. He allowed some of the recent scandals in nationally known Christian ministries to go on for years before surfacing in the media. Sooner or later, however, sin will pay you back. For someone who is in denial—and this is axiomatic—life will always get worse before it gets better, unless there is repentance and change. But this is why denial is so subtly self-destructive, because it will not allow you to change. The apostle Paul wrote, "If we judged ourselves, we would not come under judgment" (1 Corinthians 11:31). But judging yourself, healthy self-examination, is impossible when you are bound by denial.

Denial and Spiritual Warfare

It was the evening before I first preached this message on the belt of truth. I was out jogging, thinking hard about my sermon and its implications. Suddenly the whole issue of spiritual deception hit me like a bolt of lightning. Do you know why self-deception, denial and lying are so ter-rible? Because those are the tactics of Satan himself, who is the father of lies, *and he attaches himself to dishonest people.* Denial is spiritually dangerous.

This, then, is the result of the unhappy consequences of dishonesty: *It may open you up to the direct oppression and control of the devil.* This is certainly the logic of Ephesians 6.

If our battle is not with flesh and blood, if we have an adversary who is trying to destroy us, we must shield ourselves with the armor of God. Taking up the belt of truth, the first step, keeps us out of the steel trap of self-deception, out of the clutches of Satan.

Scott Peck argues in *People of the Lie* that persistent denial may actually allow the entrance of evil spirits, which cement our sin in virtually unbreakable behavioral problems. Charlene is a case study to which he devotes a lengthy chapter. Later in the book he concludes,

> When I was working with her I felt almost overwhelmed by Charlene's sickness. I wasn't sure I had the power to cure her. Now, in fact, I know that I, alone, did not and still do not have the power and that the psychoanalytic method I used was not wholly the right approach to her. Then I knew no other way to go. Today is different. I do know another approach, far more appropriate and possibly effective in such a case. Today, if I could see evidence that a healthy part of her wanted the whole to be healed, I would with conviction and authority offer Charlene the possible means of her salvation: deliverance and exorcism (p. 181).

This is spiritual warfare.

Listen to what Paul writes to the Thessalonians: "The coming of the lawless one [the Antichrist] will be in accordance with the work of Satan displayed . . . in every sort of evil that deceives those who are perishing. They perish *because they refused to love the truth* and so be saved. For this reason God sends them a powerful delusion so that they will believe the lie" (2 Thessalonians 2:9–11). What people believe or refuse to believe about God and about themselves is influenced by the father of lies himself. Peter rebuked Ananias, "How is it that Satan has so filled your heart that you have lied to the Holy Spirit?"(Acts 5:3).

The Power of Personal Confession

You can practice personal honesty by making yourself accountable to another person you trust. You need someone to whom you can speak openly about your fears, failures and sins. Kurt Koch, author of numerous books on the occult and demonization, writes in *Christian Counseling and Occultism,*

> The taking of refuge in secrecy is a characteristic feature of the powers of darkness. . . . The demonic tempter always lives . . . by the power of the secrecy which exists between him and us. As long as there are certain things kept secret in our life, which no man may know, the crafty enemy will have dominion over our soul. As soon, however, as the secret is told and betrayed, the power of darkness loses its claim of dominion over us. Hence, confession is . . . a counter-action against the kingdom of darkness (p. 312).

I was speaking at a Youth With A Mission discipleship school in Oregon, and a young man asked if we could spend some time together. He was still reeling from the recent breakup of his church where he had served faithfully as an associate pastor for several years.

He could not free himself from obsessive thoughts about his perceived failure in his relationship with his former pastor. After talking for nearly two hours, I asked him if he would like to pray. He said yes. I asked him to echo my words as I led him in a confession of release. Suddenly, at the crucial point in the prayer of release, he became utterly mute. He was unable to repeat what I had just spoken.

It was a moment of crisis and change. He was about to be liberated from spiritual oppression. He stared at me with teary eyes and confessed, "Man, is this hard."

Taking a deep breath and fighting for his emotional life, he continued his prayer and a powerful release ensued. He was free. Personal acknowledgment and confession to me, coupled with the two of us agreeing in prayer, were the keys to his deliverance. I doubt that he could have had a similar experience on his own. "Confess your sins to each other," James wrote, "and pray for each other so that you may be healed" (5:16).

Resisting the Father of Lies

Resistance to the father of lies begins with an uncompromising, unwavering commitment to the truth and truthfulness, especially with yourself.

Listen to Paul's resolve:

> We have renounced disgraceful ways—secret thoughts, feelings, desires and underhandedness, methods and arts that men hide through shame; we refuse to deal craftily (to practice trickery and cunning) or to adulterate or handle dishonestly the Word of God; but we state the truth openly—clearly and candidly.   2 Corinthians 4:2, AMPLIFIED

Recognize that you have an adversary who specializes in lies and half-truths, and refuse to identify yourself with him and his schemes. Instead, repent. Turn away from the fig leaves of self-protection and put on the covering of

God, the belt of truth. Put on the armor of God as if your life depended on it, for it does.

A prayer for putting on the belt of truth: Dear Lord Jesus, You are the way, *the truth* and the life. I turn away from dishonesty and distortion. I put on the belt of truth. I renounce the devil, who is the father of lies. Help me to be honest with myself and with others. Let me be like Your disciple Nathaniel of whom You said, "Behold, a man in whom there is no guile." Deliver me from defensiveness and the blindness that does not let me see myself as You see me and as others see me. I recognize that the only way I will ever change is to see where I need to change. I must be honest with myself, even if it hurts, because it will hurt even more if I do not change. Forgive me for blaming others, for holding others responsible for my problems. I make me feel the way I do. I take responsibility for my feelings and behaviors. In Jesus' mighty name, Amen.

6

The Breastplate of Righteousness

Stand firm then . . . with the breastplate of righteousness in place.   Ephesians 6:14

It was the late 1960s. Our college soccer team made a road
trip to Stanford University, and there on the public mall of
a great American university I was eyewitness to the bizarre
rites we had been seeing on television. Right in front of me
was a large group of Hare Krishnas, doing their sacred
dance and offering onlookers their holy food: popcorn.

I refused their offer and continued staring. Their faces,
except for their shaven heads, looked like any other young
Americans'. Some of our guys began witnessing to them,
but they responded with religious scorn. I remember their
ridiculing my friend's athletic bag: "Why do you fool with
such nonsense?" The implication, of course, was that if we
were really interested in religion, we would abstain from
everything worldly, including sports.

Unfortunately, there are many Christians who feel the
same way. Righteousness, for them, is a list of do's and
don't's. The more carefully you define your list, the more
righteous you will be. Overuse, abuse and misconceptions
have made the term *righteousness* virtually meaningless.

More often than not it has a negative connotation. Even if we understand it correctly, righteousness is something everybody shuns: "The sinful mind is hostile to God. It does not submit to God's law, nor can it do so" (Romans 8:7).

So, in order to understand the breastplate of righteousness, we must explore the biblical concept of righteousness and its relationship to spiritual warfare. We must also learn how to overcome the temptation to sin.

What Is Righteousness?

Paul probably had Isaiah 59 in mind when he wrote about the armor of God:

> The Lord looked and was displeased that there was no justice. He . . . was appalled that there was no one to intercede; so his own arm worked salvation for him, and his own righteousness sustained him. *He put on righteousness as his breastplate,* and the helmet of salvation on his head.   Isaiah 59:15–17

The "breastplate of righteousness" originates with God Himself, which means that righteousness can be understood only in its relation to the divine nature. In fact, the whole armor of God is a revelation of the whole character of God. To study the armor of God is to study God's attributes. To put on the armor is to put on God's qualities: truth, righteousness, peace, faith and salvation.

Conversely, a study of the armor of God also opens up possibilities for a better understanding of the nature of the enemy we are fighting. Satan is a kind of spiritual anti-matter. Whatever God is, Satan isn't. God is light; Satan is darkness. God is truth and truthful; Satan is the father of lies, the great deceiver and the master of distortion. Jesus is the Prince of Peace; Satan is the underlying cause of strife and chaos. Jesus is the Author and Finisher of our faith; Satan is the proponent of unbelief. God gives salvation and life; Satan seeks to steal, kill and destroy.

With regard to righteousness, Satan's plan is to repress it and foster instead either sin and unrighteousness or false righteousness—human effort to meet the standards of God. Righteousness that is not grounded in the nature of God and imparted to us by God's grace becomes a righteousness of rules. Legalism is righteousness without relationship, regulations without love. In contrast, true righteousness flows out of our personal friendship with the Father.

Righteousness Out of Relationship

Imagine that one day your doorbell rings, and there standing on your porch are three children who offer you a shocking proposal. After shopping around the neighborhood, they have decided to ask you to become their parent, but they would like to know the rules of your household before making a final commitment. They have been searching, they tell you, for the ideal family, and they are willing to *prove* they are worthy of your love by obeying your rules. And as long as they obey the rules they expect you to love and care for them.

Strange scenario? Not really! This is the way many Christians think about their relationships with God. They would agree that He is their Father, but only conditionally. If they do what is right, they reason, God will keep loving them. If they don't, well . . . maybe He will, maybe He won't.

This is not the biblical revelation of righteousness by grace through faith. Christians are not God's children because we have impressed Him with our good works and carefully obeyed all His family rules. We are His children by birth, by being born of the Spirit. This new birth means a dramatic change in our relationship with God.

To the unbeliever, God is a judge, and a judge bases his decisions on the way the accused obeys—or disobeys—the rules; relationship is not relevant.

To the Christian, someone who has become a member of the family of God by believing in His Son, Jesus, God is a Father. For a father, relationship is the bottom line, not rules. Jesus illustrated this in the story of the Prodigal Son. The father, in overwhelming love for his sorrowful son, seemed to overlook his child's sinful choices.

True righteousness, then, is grounded in a relationship of grace. The fearsome Judge becomes our loving Father.

> Since we have now been justified by his [Jesus'] blood, how much more shall we be saved from God's wrath through him! For if, when we were God's enemies, we were reconciled to him through the death of his Son, how much more, having been reconciled, shall we be saved through his life!   Romans 5:9–10

Righteousness, therefore, is not just what we do. It is who we are. Before being saved, a person is a sinner by nature, not merely because he or she commits sin. This is why Jesus said we must be born again. In other words, we need a new nature. Jesus died not only for our *sins*, plural, but when He was crucified, our *sin nature* was nailed to the cross with Him. In this event there is a kind of legal exchange offered to those who believe in Christ. The apostle Paul put it this way: "God made [Jesus] who had no sin to be sin for us, so that in him we might become the righteousness of God" (2 Corinthians 5:21).

Righteousness, then, grounded in the nature of God, is *imputed* to [a theological term meaning "given to and placed in"] those who trust in Jesus Christ. Paul used Abraham's experience with God to illustrate this doctrine: "Abraham believed God, and it was credited to him as righteousness" (Romans 4:3). Righteousness, the very righteousness of God, is credited to our account when we first believe in Christ. Relationship with God is established—not based on what we have done, but on the legal transfer of Christ's righteousness to us.

When the Father sees us born again, impregnated with a new nature, clothed with the robe of the righteousness of Christ Himself, He receives us to Himself as one of His very own—and loves us unconditionally.

In the words of the hymn,

> *My hope is built on nothing less*
> *than Jesus' blood and righteousness.*

Shall we sin more, just so God has a chance to express His unconditional love? Of course not! That is not a part of a relationship either. I don't run around on my wife because I am free from rules. If I need a banner that says *Don't cheat on your wife*, then something is fundamentally wrong with our relationship.

Righteousness and God's Laws

What value, then, do the laws of God have for the believer? Everything. The laws are not a means of eternal salvation, but remain a revelation of God who is the Author of the law. Obedience to God's Word—righteousness—lines us up with God's order. A law will never get you to heaven. Only God's grace in Christ can do that.

But obeying the Word will keep you out of a heap of trouble.

God's Law, or God's Word, is God's authority. Thus, obedience places you under the protective covering of His authority. Disobedience does not take you, like the Prodigal Son, out of relationship with the Father, but it certainly takes you out of His home and lands you in the muddy pigpen of your own sin. Defined simply, *righteousness is doing what is right*. "Dear children," John wrote, "do not let anyone lead you astray. *He who does what is right is righteous*" (1 John 3:7).

God's Law is an order of life. The root of the Greek term *dike*, which is translated "righteousness" or "justice," means literally "to give direction, to establish." Righteousness gives your life direction and establishes it on the rock of God's character. In other words, *doing what is right is good for you! You* are the beneficiary of right living.

The Scriptures are commonly called *The Holy Bible*. Perhaps a better title would be *Father Knows Best*. God's Word does not restrict us. It saves our lives. The Bible is like a manufacturer's instruction manual. Who would think of operating an expensive piece of high-tech medical equipment without first reading the operator's guide? And yet the guidelines for human relations and relationship with God, written by the Creator Himself, are often ignored.

My wife and I have raised three children, and each one has resisted learning to look both ways before crossing the street. I have even had to punish them for ignoring my warnings. From their narrow preschool point of view, my demand was unreasonable and unfair. But why did I lay down that "law"? To restrict their freedom? Or to preserve their lives?

One of the most difficult things I face as a pastor is challenging young couples to maintain their sexual purity before marriage. At any given time, our church has twenty or more couples in our pre-marriage counseling program. Surprisingly, a large proportion of the couples who want to enter the program are already living together. Many are new Christians with unformed convictions, but many should know better. The world's way of doing things can have a powerful influence on the best of us.

In conjunction with our pre-marriage counseling, we ask couples not to live with one another. Our rationale is God's Word. We assume that if the Bible is against pre-marital sex, then abstinence is not only right, it's good for the couple's long-term relationship. And, oh, do some people object! Some even opt to be married somewhere else.

But my convictions remain firm. I have often asked couples, "What if we were living in a country where being a Christian was against the law? Suppose you received Christ, were baptized, and word reached your employer. You knew that within a week you would lose your job. If you asked me for counsel, what would you expect me to tell you as your pastor? What if I suggested, 'Don't worry. Deny Christ. You need your job to support your family. God will forgive you'? Would you trust me as your spiritual leader?"

Doing what is right is no easy road, but there are few better shields to repel the fiery darts of the enemy and help you stand strong. Like the small end of a funnel, the narrow gate, the right way, offers few options, and sometimes only one, but ultimately it leads to the broad spectrum of God's blessing and life. The wide gate is like the same funnel in reverse. It has multiple options, all of which lead to only one consequence—death (Matthew 7:13–14). There is a way that seems right to us, but the end of that way is death (Proverbs 16:25).

Even the world recognizes, infrequently and reluctantly, that right living is good for you. A newspaper article in the *Arizona Republic* (November 24, 1988, section B, p. 1) headlined recently, "Abstinence is [the] key to [a] likely revamp of sex education." It reported that the sex education proposal presented in 1988 by the State Board of Education included abstinence as the only 100 percent effective way to avoid pregnancy and sexually transmitted diseases; the promotion of honor and respect for monogamous, heterosexual marriage; and discussion of the possible emotional and psychological consequences of teens' and preteens' becoming involved in sexual intercourse.

The article was subtitled "Proposal similar to guidelines California uses." California? The home of Hollywood and free sex? Incredible? No. This is simply a rediscovery that "Father knows best." Righteousness is not restrictive. It is liberating, and doing what is right is often a matter of life and death.

If doing what is right is good for you, then failing to do the right thing—disobedience—is self-destructive and may even invite the personal participation of Satan himself in your life. The apostle Paul wrote, "As for you, you were dead in your transgressions and sins, in which you used to live when you followed the ways of this world and of the ruler of the kingdom of the air, *the spirit who is now at work in those who are disobedient* " (Ephesians 2:1–2).

Jesus taught His disciples the peril of unrighteousness. Shortly before His crucifixion He announced to them, "The prince of this world is coming. He has no hold on me" (John 14:30). Satan tempted Jesus, hoping for a replay of man's Fall in the Garden of Eden. But Jesus refused to sin and thereby give the devil a place in His life. The breastplate of righteousness is an essential defense in spiritual warfare.

Paul picks up on this idea of giving the devil a place in your life. " 'In your anger,' " he wrote, " 'do not sin.' Do not let the sun go down while you are still angry, and do not give the devil a foothold" (Ephesians 4:26–27). If we let our anger go unchecked, if we are persistently disobedient, we risk the chance of exposing ourselves to direct demonic influence. Merrill Unger, the renowned Old Testament scholar, wrote in *Demons in the World Today*, "It is possible for a believer to experience severe demon influence or obsession if he persistently yields to demonic temptation and sin" (p. 116). We *must* crucify our carnal natures and overcome temptation.

Understanding and Overcoming Temptation

Living righteously requires an understanding of the nature of temptation and how to overcome it. A master key in spiritual warfare is recognizing the part you play, because temptation really starts with you! Binding the devil is directly related to restraining yourself. As we saw earlier, the apostle Peter commands us to be sober and vigilant, "self-controlled and alert" (1 Peter 5:8). Why? Because our adversary the devil is prowling around like a roaring lion, looking for someone to devour. Jesus once told Peter, "Satan hath desired to have you" (Luke 22:31, KJV). Restrain yourself and resist the devil.

What goes through your mind when you are tempted? What do you do about it? How do you handle yourself? If you are like most people, you are not just influenced by the temptation itself. The moment you are put on trial by some external temptation, the inner you becomes a tangle of misdirected thoughts and wrong responses. What happens on the outside is secondary to what happens on the inside.

You may be tempted sexually, or by materialism, but those kinds of things only bring out the real you. Like Adam and Eve, our real problem is not with the forbidden fruit, but with ourselves. And this is precisely the emphasis in James 1:12–16:

> Blessed is the man who perseveres under trial, because when he has stood the test, he will receive the crown of life that God has promised to those who love him. When tempted, no one should say, "God is tempting me." For God cannot be tempted by evil, nor does he tempt anyone; but each one is tempted when, by his own evil desire, he is dragged away and enticed. Then, after desire has conceived, it gives birth to sin; and sin, when it is full-grown, gives birth to death.

There are three significant principles in this passage.

One: Take Personal Responsibility (Verse 12)

In order to overcome temptation and resist the devil, you must take responsibility for your attitudes and behaviors. We cannot control what happens to us, but by God's grace we can control our responses.

A friend of mine and I were discussing the untimely death of a Christian woman. She was young and full of faith—disturbingly full of faith, because anyone with as much faith as she seemed to have had just shouldn't die!

I will never forget what my friend mumbled to me in the deathly quiet of the church foyer the day of her funeral: *"Victorious Christian living is not coming to someplace in life where you don't have anymore problems."* No one can avoid the temptation to sin or to give up on God. Rather, victory in Christ means that we can be more than conquerors right in the middle of the problem. Whether or not the problem or temptation goes away, we must cling tenaciously to Jesus.

I cannot always control circumstances or their ultimate outcome. I cannot always choose what happens to me. But I can choose my attitudes and behaviors in the face of what happens.

Two: Don't Blame Others (Verse 13)

It is impossible, though, to take personal responsibility if I continue to hold others responsible for my situation. Jesus was a victim who did not allow Himself to be victimized. He did not try to control those who crucified Him, although He could have called a legion of angels to His defense. He chose instead to control His response: "Father, forgive them, for they do not know what they are doing" (Luke 23:34). When He was reviled, He did not revile back, but committed everything to the Father (see 1 Peter 2:23). Jesus took personal responsibility for His feelings, and He refused to blame anyone else for what was happening to Him. He didn't even blame His heavenly Father, although He knew it was the Father's will for Him to die.

I will say it again: It is impossible to take personal responsibility for your feelings and behaviors if you blame others. This is the heart of what James is saying in 1:13: "When tempted, no one should say, 'God is tempting me.' For God cannot be tempted by evil, nor does He tempt anyone." God is not the one who tempts us. Jesus even taught us to pray to the Father, "Lead us not into temptation, but deliver us from the evil one" (Matthew 6:13).

The-devil-made-me-do-it philosophy of life is *not* biblical either. In fact, this is one of Satan's schemes. If he can get you to blame him for your inability to resist temptations, then he has gained a great victory. He is more than willing to take the blame if it means you will not change. If you don't take responsibility for your response to the temptation, you will never overcome it. Be self-controlled and alert, for your adversary the devil, like a roaring lion, is on the hunt.

In *Why Am I Afraid to Tell You Who I Am?*, bestselling author John Powell tells the story of the syndicated columnist Sydney Harris, who once accompanied a friend of his to the newsstand.

> Accepting the newspaper which was shoved rudely in his direction, the friend of Harris politely smiled and wished the newsman a nice weekend. As the two friends walked down the street, the columnist asked:
> "Does he always treat you so rudely?"
> "Yes, unfortunately, he does."
> "And are you always so polite and friendly to him?"
> "Yes, I am."
> "Why are you so nice to him when he is so unfriendly to you?"
> "Because I don't want *him* to decide how I'm going to act," his friend replied. "I'm not going to allow the way he acts to determine how I feel inside or how I respond" (pp. 38–39).

We cannot always control what happens to us. We will be tempted to sin, but we must take personal responsibility for our feelings and behaviors. Don't blame God. He tempts no one. Don't blame the devil. He doesn't *make* you do anything. And don't blame others. Don't even blame yourself. Paul wrote to the Corinthians, "I care very little if I am judged by you or by any human court; *indeed, I do not even judge myself.* My conscience is clear . . ." (1 Corinthians 4:3–4).

There is a great difference between blaming yourself and taking responsibility. It is one thing to say, "I'm going to make the best of this situation." It's quite another to say, "Poor me. I'm such a terrible person. My failure brought this on."

Self-pity is nothing more than emotional penance. Flagellating yourself with poor-me's will not heal your soul. That can actually be just another subtle way to avoid taking personal responsibility for your feelings and behaviors.

No one makes me feel the way I do—not the guy at the newsstand, not my wife, not my children, not my neighbor, not my boss. Not even the devil! *I* make me feel the way I do. And it is impossible for me to overcome temptation if I am blind to myself. Therein lies the mastery of the tempter, which is why James writes, "But each one is tempted when, by his own evil desire, he is dragged away and enticed" (James 1:14).

Three: Understand Yourself and the Nature of Temptation (Verses 14–15)

Temptation begins with an unwillingness to take personal responsibility for our feelings and behaviors. Temptation without human weakness is like a seed without water. Bait is not the reason fish bite. It's because they are hungry. "Each one is tempted when, by his own evil desire, he is dragged away and enticed" (James 1:14). My battle is not with temptation, but with myself.

The Greek term used here, *epithumia*, translated "evil desire" or "lust," can be misleading because it can be used in either a positive or negative sense. It means, more accurately, "great desire." Jesus used the term with reference to the Last Supper when He said, "I have *eagerly desired* to eat this Passover with you before I suffer" (Luke 22:15).

Paul also used the term in a powerfully positive sense when he wrote, "I *desire* to depart and be with Christ, which is better by far" (Philippians 1:23). In other words, we cannot assume that James' use of *epithumia* is necessarily negative. In fact, the context seems to bear this out. According to James, *epithumia*—strong desire—is not sin unless "desire has conceived" (1:15). My point is that a strong desire is not in itself sin. Our human passions are the target of temptation, but sin occurs only when we succumb to the temptation and surrender our will to the passions of the flesh.

Christians may never call their feelings "sinful," but what we say about our feelings suggests otherwise. I do not know how many people have apologized to me for crying during a counseling session. I often have to tell people that it's O.K. to cry. I have to remind them that Jesus felt deep emotion, too.

The shortest verse in the Bible is one of the most touching: "Jesus wept." We have a High Priest who feels what we feel, who hurts when we hurt and who holds us in His arms when we cry. "Blessed are those who mourn, for they shall be comforted." My passions and desires are not evil unless I use them for sinful purposes.

When *epithumia* becomes sin, it opens up all kinds of possibilities for evil. Sin, James writes, when it has become "full grown," results in death. It is one thing into sin, to give in to your passions momentarily quite another to give yourself over to the lusts of the flesh, where sin becomes a behavior pattern.

An occasional trespass is relatively easy to overcome, but habits of sin are very difficult to break, and they invariably lead to death. James is using the term *death*, I believe, in its inclusive sense—death in all its forms: spiritual and physical, emotional and relational. "There is a way that seems right to a man, but in the end it leads to death" (Proverbs 14:12).

Listen to what Paul wrote to Timothy in this regard:

> Those who oppose him [the Lord's servant] he must gently instruct, in the hope that God will grant them repentance leading them to a knowledge of the truth, and that they will come to their senses and escape from the trap of the devil, who has taken them captive to do his will.   2 Timothy 2:25

When people reject the truth and give in to temptation, they "undress" themselves. Without the breastplate of righteousness, we stand naked before the devil. Without a firm commitment to resist temptation, we risk becoming spiritual captives, bound to our patterns of sin and bound to the devil to do his will.

Finally, and probably most importantly, we have a High Priest, the Lord Jesus, who understands our temptations and is touched by the feelings of our weaknesses. He was tempted just as we are, and "because he himself suffered when he was tempted, he is able to help those who are being tempted" (Hebrews 2:18).

Jesus understands what you are facing.

Jesus feels what you are feeling.

Jesus wants to help you endure temptation and over-come it.

> The night is nearly over; the day is almost here. So let us put aside the deeds of darkness and put on the armor of light. . . . Clothe yourselves with the Lord Jesus Christ, and do not think about how to gratify the desires of the sinful nature.   Romans 13:12–14

A prayer for putting on the breastplate of righteousness: Heavenly Father, righteous God, I thank You that my re-lationship with You is based on the righteousness of Your Son, Jesus. I stand in Your grace. I could never be good enough in myself to come to You, or to stand against the devil. Thank You, Lord, for the righteousness of Christ deposited into my heavenly bank account. I make a with-drawal to take care of my needs today. I stand shielded by the breastplate of Your perfect and permanent righteous-ness. I am also determined to honor Your laws, to obey Your Word and to do what is right. In the name of Jesus, I resist the temptation to sin, to enter the wide gate, to walk down the path of least resistance, to do what is wrong. In the name of Jesus, I resist the devil, the one who has been breaking Your laws from the beginning. You, God, are my righteousness, and I will live in obedi-ence to Your Word. You are My Father, and You know best. In Jesus' mighty name, Amen.

7

The Readiness of Peace

Stand firm then . . . with your feet fitted with the
readiness that comes from the gospel of peace.
Ephesians 6:14–15

As a pastor I find, without a doubt, that the greatest challenge of full-time ministry is people. Our church staff has often joked, tongue-in-cheek, "If we didn't have so many people around here, we wouldn't have all these problems."

I have tried to ward off church strife by pasting Romans 14:19 on my office door: "Let us therefore *make every effort* to do what leads to peace and to mutual edification." I prefer no one enter my office without first coming under the authority of that Scripture. I wish I could say it works!

People, even pastors and church leaders, are generally unaware of the dramatic impact their attitudes and negative words can have on others. The writer of Hebrews warns us, "See to it . . . that no bitter root grows up to cause trouble and defile many" (Hebrews 12:15).

But here is the stinger. People are even less aware that their attitudes—and their "sincere and honest" comments that release those attitudes—may actually be influenced by demons. The Bible presents this as a possibility. The "wisdom" of "bitter envy and selfish ambition," James writes, "does not come down from heaven but is earthly, unspiritual, *of the devil* . . . [and] there you find disorder and every evil practice" (James 3:14–16). Maybe this is why James also writes earlier in his letter, "'Everyone should be quick to listen, slow to speak and slow to become angry" (James 1:19).

Sometimes even well-meaning words, ill-timed and thoughtlessly spoken, can have the bite of a scorpion. When Jesus predicted His death, Peter reacted with all the best intentions. "You'll never die, Lord. I won't let that happen, even if I have to give up my own life for You." Jesus recognized instantly the demonic source of Peter's impetuous remark: "Out of my sight, Satan! You are a stumbling block to me; you do not have in mind the things of God, but the things of men" (Matthew 16:23).

Not every divisive attitude or comment is devilish, but many are. This is why Paul expects every believer to have his feet "fitted with the readiness that comes from the gospel of peace," so that we will be able to stand up and fight "when the day of evil comes." We have to learn how to make peace, not war.

Now this may seem to contradict the very message of this book: spiritual warfare. But listen again carefully to our key verse: "Our warfare is *not* with flesh and blood." In other words, God's command to believers is to stand and fight the devil, not one another. We actually resist the devil and his schemes when we keep the unity of the Spirit in the bond of peace.

While Satan is aggressively making war, we must be aggressively making peace. Peace is part of the full armor of God, and there are three important terms in Ephesians 6:15 that bear our attention: *the gospel of peace, readiness* and *feet.*

The Gospel of Peace

The gospel of peace is, simply, the good news of peace. The Greek word translated *gospel* means "good message." *Evangelist*, which means "messenger of good," is an English word derived from this same Greek term. Specifically, the Gospel is the good news of peace with God through Jesus Christ. "Glory to God in the highest, and *on earth peace* . . . " was the heavenly anthem heralded that first Christmas (Luke 2:14).

The biblical idea of peace is comprehensive. It includes peace of mind, but there is much more. Peace in the Bible has to do ultimately with our relationship with God. Personal wholeness begins only when we are reconciled to God. Sin is a declaration of war. The death of Christ on the cross was God's offer of peace. Jesus actually took the blame for our sin, and when we come to Him in faith, our wrong standing with God is made right.

"Since we have been justified through faith, we have peace with God through our Lord Jesus Christ" (Romans 5:1). Thus, the healing of our broken relationship with the Father is the most important kind of peace. It is the restoration of *shalom*, the common but comprehensive Hebrew term translated "peace." The *Theological Wordbook of the Old Testament* describes *shalom* as follows:

> The general meaning behind the root *sh-l-m* is of completion and fulfillment—of entering into a state of wholeness and unity, a restored relationship. . . . [It means] peace, prosperity, health, completeness, safety (Vol. II, p. 930–931).

Shalom is everything that is right. It could even be said that the word *shalom* in the Old Testament took on messianic overtones. The Jews would never realize true peace, security, wholeness and even national restoration until the coming of the Messiah to establish God's Kingdom in the earth. Satan has made war on the saints, but God's Kingdom will prevail. Isaiah prophesied,

> For to us a child is born . . . and the government will be on his shoulders. And he will be called . . . Prince of Peace [shalom]. Of the increase of his government and peace [shalom] there will be no end. He will reign on David's throne . . . upholding it with justice and righteousness from that time on and forever.
>
> Isaiah 9:6–7

Shalom is everything that's right. Shalom is everything right with God. Shalom is also everything right in my relationships with others. "Implicit in *shalom* is the idea of unimpaired relationships with others" (*Theological Wordbook of the Old Testament,* p. 931).

Here is where we cross the line and the real battles of daily life begin—in relationships. Satan will do everything in his power to keep us out of relationship with God. Once we are justified and have peace with God, the devil will do everything in his power to keep us out of relationship with one another. It took a mighty act of God to make peace with us. It will take all of our might, empowered by the Holy Spirit, to keep peace with others.

Healthy relationships are not just part of being a Christian; they are crucial. How can we say we love God, whom we have not seen, if we cannot love our brother whom we have seen (1 John 4:20)? And Jesus taught that if we come to the place of prayer and remember that something is not right in a relationship with someone else, we are to leave religious devotion behind us, make things right with the brother, and then return to the place of prayer (see Matthew 5:23–24). God does not want our "religion" if it does not radically change the way we relate to other people in our lives.

Peacemaking restores the image of God, something of which many Christians have only a general understanding. Genesis 1:26–27 is the basic revelation of the image of God:

> Then God said, "Let us make man in our image, in our likeness, and let them rule. . . ." So God created man in his own image, in the image of God he created him; male and female he created them.

Notice first the multiple references to plurality or community within the Godhead: "Let *us* make man in *our* image, in *our* likeness." This is the Trinity in consultation.

Furthermore, the Hebrew term *elohim* translated "God" here in Genesis 1:26 and throughout the Old Testament is, strangely, a plural form, also suggesting the Trinity. *Elohim* literally means "gods." The great, fundamental doctrine of Judaism has always been, "The Lord [YHWH] our God [Elohim], the Lord is one" (Deuteronomy 6:4), and yet the basic Hebrew word for *God* is plural!

In Genesis 1, Elohim purposes to create man in His image, in the image of the plurality of His triune Being. "Let *us* make man in *our* image, in *our* likeness." The image of the community of the Trinity has been stamped on the community of humanity. The image of God, then, is relationship in community. This is further affirmed in the unusual and often unnoticed statement of Genesis 1:27: "In the image of God he created him; *male and female*." Or, to paraphrase, "In His image Elohim created human persons as a community of relational, interdependent beings."

Theologian Millard Erickson writes in Volume 1 of *Christian Theology*,

> The teaching regarding the image of God in man has also been viewed as an intimation of the Trinity. Genesis 1:27 reads:
>
> > So God created man in his own image,
> > in the image of God he created him;
> > male and female he created them.
>
> Some would argue that what we have here is a parallelism not merely in the first two, but in all three lines. Thus, "male and female he created them" is equivalent to "So God created man in his own image" and to "in the image of God he created him." On this basis, the image of God in man (generic) is to be found in the fact that man has been created male and female (i.e., plural). This means that the image of God must consist in a unity in plurality (p. 329).

This is not to say, of course, that the male/female relationship is the only relationship between two human beings that has real meaning. "Male/female" is simply an ultimate model of mutual interdependence and unity in differentiation. In the union of male and female, the two become *one flesh*. The apostle Paul calls this one flesh relationship of husband and wife "a great mystery" (Ephesians 5:31–32).

Out of His image, God has given to us the most precious thing about Himself—the harmonious, loving, consummate oneness that He experiences with His own Being. The most sacred thing we have as human beings, outside of our relationship with God, is our relationship with one another. *The image of God is our co-humanity.**

We are mutually dependent on one another, just as there is a mutual dependence among the Persons of the God-head. No man is an island—this God has ordained forever by permanently imprinting His image of interdependence on us, His special creatures. In all of God's creation, only man fully understands and experiences true relationships. Walter Brueggemann, a Methodist theologian, writes in *Genesis: A Bible Commentary for Teaching and Preaching,*

> On the one hand, humankind is a single entity. All human persons stand in solidarity before God. But on the other hand, humankind is a community, male and female. And none is the full image of God alone. Only in community of humankind is God reflected. God is, according to this bold affirmation [Genesis 1:27], not mirrored as an individual, but as a community (p. 34).

The great biblical term to describe the relational interaction between God and man, and person to person, is *love.* In *Foundations of Dogmatics* (Vol. 1) German theologian Otto Weber writes,

> To put it another way, man is in the "image of God" in his predetermination to be one who loves. But he cannot love God without seeing his "neighbor" as destined to be a co-partner in God's covenant and to love him as such. Being-based-upon-God can never be anything other than being-for-the-other-person (p. 574).

---

* There are other popular definitions of the image of God. It is often deduced, for example, that unique aspects of human life, like creativity, rationality, morality, are images of God in us.

God is love, and love makes peace. God loved the world so much that He gave His only begotten Son to make peace with us (John 3:16). "This is how we know what love is: Jesus Christ laid down his life for us. And we ought to lay down our lives for our brothers" (1 John 3:16).

In terrible contrast, Satan is hate, and hate makes war. It is still his singular purpose to bring strife and division into every level of human society, from the small unit of the home to great international conflicts. Our spiritual enemy champions the disruption of relationships. The angels rejoice in heaven when one person is saved. The demons rejoice in hell when a marriage ends in divorce, or when a church is fragmented by strife. Satan's hateful plan is to destroy the thing in us most precious to God—His image.

Created to be a community of love, man has become a world of prejudice and hate. But Jesus "himself is our peace, who has . . . destroyed the barrier, the dividing wall of hostility [between Jews and Gentiles, among everyone]. . . . His purpose was to create in himself one new man out of the two, thus making peace, and in this one body to reconcile both of them to God through the cross, by which he put to death their hostility" (Ephesians 2:14–17).

The great conflict, then, is between Satan and the Prince of Peace, between those who sow strife and those who make peace. As C. S. Lewis wrote in his essay "Christianity and Culture," "There is no neutral ground in the universe: Every square inch, every split second, is claimed by God and counterclaimed by Satan." The image of God, then, will either be tarnished or polished, damaged or restored.

Readiness

Returning now to Ephesians 6:15, the second important term is *readiness*. Strife and division, the things that erode relationships, seem to occur naturally. You really don't have to look for a fight. One will come your way whether or not you want it. In one of the lesser quoted "promises" of the Bible, Jesus said, "Things that cause people to sin are bound to come" (Luke 17:1). He was not being negative, He was being realistic about life.

Problems just happen. Peace doesn't. Peace is elusive. Peace happens because someone makes it happen. Peace is something you have to work on. You have to take the initiative. If for no other reason, we know this because it is the basic message of the Gospel. God Himself took the initiative to make peace. He was in Christ, reconciling the world to Himself (2 Corinthians 5:19), and we have been commissioned with the ministry of reconciliation. "Blessed are the peace*makers*, for they will be called sons of God" (Matthew 5:9).

The big question is: How can we *make* peace? How can we be ready? Larry Lea, author of several books on prayer, has spoken about his early morning preparation for each day. He sees the Lord's Prayer as a model prayer, a format for daily communion with God. When we pray, "Forgive us our sins, as we forgive others," we prepare ourselves *in advance* for whatever offenses the day ahead may bring. This is just another way to fit our feet with peace.

The key word here is *forgiveness*. We make peace by being prepared to forgive. What separates me from God? Sin. What isolates me from other people? Offenses. What is the correct response? The gospel of peace, forgiveness. Forgiveness is the power that restores broken relationships between God and man, and man and man. It is because of forgiveness that God accepts me the way I am. Forgiveness opens the door of reconciliation. It is through forgiveness that we make peace.

Sin separates me from God, but God's forgiveness separates my sin from me—as far as the east is from the west! When God looks at me, He actually sees me without sin. Forgiving others works much the same way. I must release them from what they have done to offend me. When I look at the offender, I must see the person and not the sin.

Impossible? Jesus once told His disciples that forgiveness was absolutely necessary, even if a person sinned against them and repented seven times in one day. Seven times in one day! Most of us can scarcely forgive seven times in a year. When the disciples are confronted with this overwhelming challenge, they cry out in desperation, "Increase our faith!" (See Luke 17:1–5.) The point here is that forgiveness is not a natural human virtue. We need divine intervention and grace to forgive.

No one ever said forgiveness would be easy. In fact, forgiveness comes only through sacrifice. I have to give up something of myself—my anger, my thirst for vengeance, my humiliation, my pride—in order to forgive. Just remember, *Jesus gave up everything*. "Bear with each other and forgive whatever grievances you may have against one another. *Forgive as the Lord forgave you*" (Colossians 3:13).

Forgive we must. Jesus told a parable of a man who refused to forgive a little offense, after his master had forgiven him an insurmountable debt. And his master was very angry, "and delivered him to the tormentors" (Matthew 18:34, KJV). Emotional torment, even spiritual oppression, is the consequence of unforgiveness, but forgiveness and reconciliation bring peace.

Feet

The third important term in Ephesians 6:15 is *feet*. We have seen that believers have been given a Kingdom com-

mission. Frequently in the Bible, the idea of spiritual authority is suggested by the term *feet*. This was a common
expression of dominion in the ancient world, as a conquer-
ing king would literally place his foot on the neck of his
vanquished foe.

Psalm 8 states clearly God's purpose for man: to have dominion, which is followed by the statement that God has
placed all things "under his feet." The Old Testament predicts that dominion, lost in Eden, will be restored through
the coming of the Messiah. He is the One whose foot will
crush the head of Satan (Genesis 3:15), and Jehovah says of
the Christ, "Sit at my right hand until I make your enemies
a footstool for your feet" (Psalm 110:1).*

Playing on the same figure of speech, Jesus announces
to His disciples that they have the authority to walk over
serpents and scorpions, and over all the power of the enemy (Luke 10:18–19). Finally, the Church as the Body of
Christ has everything under her feet as well (Ephesians
1:22–23).

My conclusion, then, is that "feet fitted with the readiness of the gospel of peace" is a veiled reference to the
source of the believer's authority. *There is spiritual authority
in peacemaking.* When the devil turns up the heat of hatred,
making peace is like aiming a fire hose at a match. There
is peace in God's authority, and there is authority in God's
peace. Isaiah proclaimed,

> The fruit of righteousness will be peace;
>   the effect of righteousness will be quietness and
>   confidence forever.

---

* This psalm, incidentally, is cited in the New Testament more often
than any other Old Testament passage. See, for example, Acts 2:33–35.

My people will live in peaceful dwelling places,
   in secure homes,
   in undisturbed places of rest.
Though hail flattens the forest
   and the city is leveled completely,
how blessed you will be,
   sowing your seed by every stream.

Isaiah 32:17–20

Peace At Any Price?

Peace at any price is what counselors call co-dependency. A woman who is married to an alcoholic, for example, can fall easily into this snare. She is always making peace with an angry man who refuses to take responsibility for his life. She tolerates his intolerable behavior and even thinks it is her fault. She may actually allow her husband to brutalize her under the guise of Christian submission.

The cross of Christ was not a doormat. The way of the cross is aggressive self-sacrifice with the singular goal of helping others.* Co-dependency (another term is *enmeshment*) never helps anyone. John wrote, "Jesus would not entrust himself to them, for he knew all men" (2:24). Jesus gave Himself *for* the people, but He would not give Himself *to* the people. With all His love, He still kept His distance.

Jesus did not love in order to get love. He loved because He was love. Co-dependency is loving to be loved, loving to meet a need in yourself, instead of loving to meet a need in the other person. The same thing can be said

---

* In contrast, the way of the world is aggressive self-preservation, which exhibits itself in aggressive behavior.

about peacemaking. Peace at any price is when I make peace for the sake of my own peace. Peace at any price is like the person with a gun to his head who shouts, "I'll do anything you want if you don't kill me." Jesus calls us to be peacemakers, not because peacemaking is a magical way to avoid the pain of life, but because it is right.

> Do not repay anyone evil for evil. Be careful to do what is right in the eyes of everybody. If it is possible, *as far as it depends on you*, live at peace with everyone.
> Romans 12:17–18

A prayer for fitting your feet with the readiness of peace: Loving Father, thank You that I am at peace with You, and that I can come to You confidently because of what Jesus has done. I pray now for peace in my soul, for Your peace, not the false and temporary peace of the world. I pray for the peace that passes all understanding. I also pray for the strength and grace to be a peacemaker. I will prepare myself now for the unexpected today, tonight and tomorrow. I forgive—in advance—those who will sin against me. I want to respond in love, not react in anger. I will make every effort, as far as it is in my ability to do so, to live at peace with everyone. I resist the prince of darkness and his snare of strife. I recognize how destructive strife can be, and I stand against it. I place myself under the Lordship of the Prince of Peace. In Jesus' mighty name, Amen.

8

The Shield of Faith

In addition to all this, take up the shield of faith, with which you can extinguish all the flaming arrows of the evil one.   Ephesians 6:16

Life is full of flaming arrows. Getting pierced with a sharp object is terrifying enough, but Paul intensifies the image by referring to arrows as being hot as a branding iron. The idea, of course, is derived from the ancient military practice of shooting a barrage of ignited arrows in order to terrorize the enemy and disrupt his ranks. A sure defense was a water-soaked leather shield. Paul calls this the shield of faith.

Without faith it is *impossible* to please God, and without faith it is *impossible* to keep standing in the heat of the battle. Yet at times it seems equally *impossible* to define faith! What is faith?

Elements of Faith

Faith is trust and confidence in another to do what you cannot do yourself. In the Bible, faith means belief and trust in God. Faith, as it is used in the New Testament, has at least four different shades of meaning.

The first of these is *saving faith*. Saving faith is the trust we place in Christ to save us from our sin and its consequences. We are saved by faith in God, as opposed to being saved by our works. Faith is a renunciation of our own works. It is an attitude that says, "My righteousness is, at best, seriously inadequate."

In what is one of the better-known passages in the New Testament, Paul wrote, "For it is by grace you have been saved, *through faith*—and this not from yourselves, it is the gift of God—not by works, so that no one can boast" (Ephesians 2:8–9). Abraham is a great example of saving faith. He "believed God, and it was credited to him as righteousness" (Romans 4:3).

The second aspect of faith is what I call *fruit faith*. Faith is listed as one of the fruits of the Spirit in Galatians 5:22–23. Interestingly, the common Greek word for faith (*pistis*) in this verse is translated "faithfulness" in most modern versions. Faith is not only the key that opens the door of salvation, it is a way of life. Faith in this sense is our daily trust in God for His help and provision.

Third, the New Testament teaches the need for a special release of faith in particular situations. This is *power faith* or *gift faith* or *miracle-working faith*. The Weymouth translation calls this "special faith" (1 Corinthians 12:9).

It is noteworthy that "faith" is the only term appearing both as a fruit of the Spirit (Galatians 5:22–23) and as a gift of the Spirit (1 Corinthians 12:7–11). This alone should tell us that there are different aspects of faith. It is quite obvious from the teaching of Paul on the spiritual gifts (1 Corinthians 12–14) that not everyone has "power faith" all the time. On the other hand, everyone must have faith in the general sense—faith to be saved and faith to walk with God. (See Hebrews 11:6.)

My fourth category is *enduring faith*. Enduring faith is the kind of faith that does not quit, especially when you feel the most like quitting. Jesus said, "Be faithful, even to the point of death, and I will give you the crown of life" (Revelation 2:10).

The Shield of Faith

The shield of faith is a reference to this last aspect of faith—steadfastness and endurance. Why? Because the subject of Ephesians 6 is not salvation, nor is it daily Christian living. Ephesians 6 is about wrestling with the devil. Enduring faith is the persistent, resilient belief that God's Word is true, over and against every problem, wrong thought or demon.

Enduring faith is wonderfully exemplified by Wycliffe missionaries Pat and Gail Burns, who are working on translating the Bible into the primitive language of Mese. After completing two years of graduate training in linguistics and after agreeing to a *fifteen-year* commitment, they relocated, little children and all, to the remote jungles of New Guinea.

Our church assists with their support, so we hear from them regularly. In a recent letter, Gail reported that their young daughter

> Laura had her first malaria attack . . . but medication took care of it promptly. It has continued to be unusually, and unseasonably, rainy here, which has caused food shortages for the people. . . . We have requested prayer, and this last week the weather patterns appear to have changed. . . . This letter is being hand-carried out to Lae. Our airstrip has been closed for several weeks, but with

improved weather, we are expecting work to be done on it soon so that it can be re-opened. We praise the Lord that we have not had medical emergencies during this time.

Pat and Gail know a level of sacrifice and commitment that few of us will ever experience. They have also encountered unusual spiritual resistance. But their letters are always cheerful, and they keep on pressing forward to the mark of their high calling in Jesus.

Theirs is not the "ordinary faith" of daily Christian living, nor is it power faith, although they certainly need both of these aspects of faith, too! Instead, their faith *endures* in the face of uncommon difficulty and intense testing. Their faith is a shield in the battle. Without it, they would not survive.

There is no formula for faith in a crisis. Faith is not a magic escape. Enduring faith is a dogged determination to rise above the injustices and pains of life, without allowing the flaming arrows of hurt and resentment to penetrate your soul. Life hurts. Faith looks to God and refuses to give those hurts a foothold in your heart. By faith we are saved. By faith we walk with God. By faith we move mountains. Under the shield of faith, held resolutely above us, we resist the devil and endure the evil day.

Faith and Endurance

"The testing of your faith develops perseverance" (James 1:3). The Greek word translated "perseverance" in this verse is *hypomone*. It is a combination of two Greek words, *meno* and *hypo*, which together mean "to remain under." The shield of faith is the ability to remain under

the fire of a long, drawn-out trial without breaking down
or blowing up. In the ancient Greek world, the word referred to "a prominent virtue in the sense of courageous
endurance," according to Kittel's *Theological Dictionary*.
"As distinct from patience, it has the active significance of
energetic if not necessarily successful resistance."

Just last month, at a Christian retreat center, I met a
woman who has been confined to a wheelchair since being
shot in a store robbery in 1971. As she passed by my open
guestroom door, her eye caught me pounding on my lap-
top computer. Turning her chair into my room, she asked
me about my writing project (this book!).

As we talked, I was surprised at her openness. She had
suffered immeasurably, not only from her disability, but at
the hands of well-meaning Christians who through the
years had dumped on her every imaginable inappropriate
comment. Often she had wished the paralyzing bullet had
taken her life. And yet there she was, at a Christian retreat, not just surviving, but diligently seeking God about
her future in full-time Christian ministry.

We are what we decide to be in the face of life's most
difficult times. Enduring faith is energetic resistance, no
matter what the outcome, no matter how long the devil
continues to fire hot darts at our souls. The opposite
of enduring faith is short-term faith, giving up and giving in.

A friend of mine played high school and college football. He once told me that one of his team's conditioning
drills was to catch automobile tires, rolled down a hill at
them by a somewhat fiendish coaching staff. It took endurance to face that day after day! Paul wrote to Timothy,
"Endure hardship with us like a good soldier of Christ
Jesus" (2 Timothy 2:3). Endurance is not a negative or

passive word. Endurance is active faith, deflecting persistently the fiery attacks of Satan.

Enduring Faith and the Nature of God

Endurance is godliness, because endurance originates with God. God is the Champion of endurance! God endures from everlasting to everlasting. In Psalm 102:12 we read, "But you, O Lord, sit enthroned forever; your renown endures through all generations." In one sense, God reigns because God endures. He "survives" every battle, every age, every generation. When you wake up tomorrow morning, God will still be there, and God will still be God. Everything about God endures: His love (Psalm 136), His name (Psalm 72:17) and His Word (Isaiah 40:8).

Jesus is the revelation of God the Father to us, and He, too, is the same yesterday and today and forever (Hebrews 13:8). If you are having difficulty holding up your shield of faith, "consider him who *endured* such opposition from sinful men, so that you will not grow weary and lose heart" (Hebrews 12:3). To endure, then, is to reign over life's problems. To quit is to allow life's problems to reign over you.

To endure is to win. The one "who stands firm to the end will be saved" (Matthew 24:13). This is not just referring to the inconvenience of a long checkout line at the grocery store, or spending the weekend with your in-laws. Jesus was speaking of enduring in the face of the absolutely worst-case scenario—the fiery days of the Great Tribulation.

How is it possible to endure to the end, especially when the trial seems endless? One day at a time! God has created us with the physical and spiritual capacity to live one day at a time, no more. His mercies are new *every morning*. Give us *this day* our *daily* bread. Take no thought about tomorrow, because there are enough troubles *today*.

There have been times when I have said to myself, "Tomorrow at this time, next week at this time, one year from today, things will be very different. I may not even remember what happened to me today." This is a simple reminder to view life from God's perspective. For Him, a day is like a thousand years, and a thousand years are like a day. The more you enter the eternal, the more you realize the temporality of your problems. Paul declared,

> We do not lose heart. . . . For our light and momentary troubles ["little" things, like being beaten, shipwrecked, imprisoned] are achieving for us an eternal glory that far outweighs them all. So we fix our eyes not on what is seen, but on what is unseen. For what is seen is temporary, but what is unseen is eternal.
> 2 Corinthians 4:16–18

Weeping may endure for a night, but joy will come in the morning (Psalm 30:5).

The Shield of Faith and the Power of God

First Peter 1:3–9 is a great summary of the concepts in this chapter: "Through faith [you] are *shielded* by God's power" (verse 5). It is not our faith that shields us. It is God's power. We often speak of the power of faith, but that can be terribly misleading. Our power is not in our faith, *per se*, but in God who is the object of our faith. "In *this* [this power of God] you greatly rejoice" (verse 6). I cannot rejoice, precisely speaking, in the troubles of life. No testing *seems* pleasant, but painful (Hebrews 12:11). I rejoice instead in the power of God to shield me and sustain me.

I also rejoice because the troubles of life give my faith an opportunity to grow. Peter continues, "All kinds of trials . . . have come so that your faith—of greater worth than gold, which perishes even though refined by fire—may be proved genuine." Suffering stretches and refines our faith. Difficult times drive us away from self-trust and toward God. The shield of faith is God's power and presence protecting and energizing us in spiritual warfare.

Finally, according to the reading of the King James Version, the shield of faith is "above all" (Greek: "in all"). Faith in the sense of perseverance shields all the other armor. Truth must persevere to prevail. Righteousness must persevere to prevail. We must persevere in peacemaking in order to prevail. And, as we will see in the next chapter, every thought becomes obedient to Christ only when we persistently resist the strongholds of the mind.

A prayer for holding up the shield of faith: Heavenly Father and mighty God, shield me with Your power as I trust in You. The flaming arrows of the enemy have burned my soul. Heal the pain inside and give me the strength to resist. I am committed to enduring to the end of this trial, regardless of how long it lasts. I am not a victim. I am a victor, more than a conqueror through Christ. My faith, Lord, is in You. I renounce my own abilities, and I confess that unless Jesus builds up my life, everything I do is in vain. Only when I trust You completely am I completely protected from the fiery darts of the wicked one. I hide myself in the fire of Your presence. In Jesus' name, Amen.

9

The Helmet of Salvation

Take the helmet of salvation.   Ephesians 6:17

It was my day off. I was doing some remodeling work at home when the phone rang. I have received my share of kooky calls, but this one deserved an award. The high-pitched, strange voice on the other end of the line asked me if I was Pastor Kinnaman.

"Yes," I admitted.

"I need someone to talk to," the voice responded.

Wondering if this was the prelude to a lengthy counseling call, I asked the ambiguous question, "Are you saved?"

"Yes," the voice replied. "I fell into my swimming pool the other day, and someone saved me."

I was speechless. I had never had that kind of response before. Then there was a short period of silence, and the mystery caller began laughing. It was a practical joke! I realized that my neighbor, who really is saved, was taking advantage of my Christian jargon and playing verbal games. "Saved" may mean any number of things, and a proper definition of *salvation* is necessary if we are to understand "the helmet of salvation."

What Is Salvation?

In the chapter on the breastplate of righteousness, I discussed the difference between "legal" righteousness, which has to do with our eternal standing with God through justification, and "practical" righteousness, our daily walk of obedience as we live out our justification. *Salvation* is another term encompassing these same two aspects. Salvation—being saved—refers to our release from sin's eternal penalty. Salvation also involves a daily process of change, whereby we grow out of our old patterns of behavior. Not only do I need right standing with God, my lifestyle needs to change, too, for my sake and for the sake of those around me.

The Greek term has a wide range of meanings, including saving, keeping, benefiting and preserving the inner being. Salvation, then, is a comprehensive term, and is most commonly understood as rescue *from* something, namely sin and its consequences, eternal death and hell on earth. But salvation is also an endowment, an impartation of divine glory. Salvation is not only an escape, it's a marvelous gift. In the Old Testament, Moses was the great deliverer. He led the people of Israel *out of* Egypt, a symbol of sin and the old life. But Joshua, whose name means "savior," led the people *into* the Promised Land. Salvation is good news and a grand exchange.

With messianic hope, Isaiah wrote,

> The Spirit of the Sovereign Lord is on me, because the Lord has anointed me to preach good news [the Gospel] to the poor. He has sent me to bind up the brokenhearted, to proclaim freedom for the captives and release [from darkness] for the prisoners, to proclaim

the year of the Lord's favor [the year of Jubilee, fig-
urative of the Messianic Kingdom] and the day of
vengeance of our God, to comfort all who mourn . . .
[and here is the grand exchange:] to bestow on them
a crown of beauty instead of ashes, the oil of gladness
instead of mourning, and a garment of praise instead
of a spirit of despair.   Isaiah 61:1–3

Not coincidentally, Jesus opened the scroll of Isaiah to
this very passage as He introduced His ministry in the
synagogue at Nazareth (see Luke 4:14–19). He is the
Anointed One, the Messiah, the Christ—the One who
makes the grand exchange possible.

The Helmet of Salvation

The term *salvation* is most commonly applied to the soul,
as in, "Fourteen *souls* were *saved* last week during our
neighborhood evangelistic campaign." Salvation is a
change of heart and nature, but it is also a change of mind.
Repentance, the way to "get saved," is the translation of a
compound Greek word, *metanoeo*, which means "change
your mind," or "change your thinking." Salvation has to
do with your head—what you think and how you think.
   "Initial" salvation changes my standing with God. The
process of salvation changes my thinking, and when I
change my thinking patterns, I change my behavior patterns. The apostle Paul wrote to the Romans, "Do not
conform any longer to the pattern of this world, but be
transformed *by the renewing of your mind*" (12:2). Change
your thoughts and you will change your life.
   Modern psychology has rediscovered the relationship of
thought and behavior. Most notably, psychologist Albert

Ellis developed what is known as the rational-emotive theory of human behavior. He identified this behavioral sequence: actuating event (*A*), belief (*B*) and consequence (*C*). Most people, he observed, connect *A* and *C* and virtually skip over *B*, as in, "That person [actuating event] *makes me* so mad [consequence]."

The fact is, no one *makes* you mad. You make yourself mad. It is what you think, your belief system (*B*) that determines how you feel and react after the actuating event. As a nationally known pastor to pastors, John Maxwell, has said, "It's not what happens *to* you, it's what happens *in* you."

The fact that we have self-control can be proven from an experience many of us relate to. Have you ever been in a hot argument with someone, your spouse perhaps, when the telephone rings? For an eternity of silent seconds you stare at each other, wondering who is going to pick up the phone. You do, and it is your employer. Your demeanor changes instantly to cheery politeness! How is it possible for you to be so angry one moment and so gracious the next? Because *you* control your emotions.

My wife and I were having a less than mild disagreement one evening when the doorbell rang. I took a deep breath, put on a mask of self-composure and opened the door. I was hoping for a salesman so I could quickly resume arguing.

But there stood my brother, grinning at me about his surprise visit. I still remember how my feelings changed, almost instantly. I tried to prevent it, but a smile broke across my face, too. I really was able to control myself. As my thoughts changed, my angry emotions subsided. My wife had not made me angry. I had made myself angry.

When I saw my brother, my thoughts changed, which changed my feelings and behavior.

I was counseling once with a young woman who had done some professional acting. She was facing a serious personal crisis and was not able to control her emotions, so she claimed. I asked her about acting. How was she able to cry when doing a sad part? "By thinking about a sad time in my life," she answered.

It was exactly the answer I was hoping to hear. "See," I told her triumphantly, "what you think really does affect the way you feel and what you do." Change your thoughts and your life will change. "Be transformed by the renewing of your mind."

Your mind is the battleground of life, and Satan knows that better than any of us. You need the helmet of salvation on your head! Your head needs salvation from wrong thoughts; immoral and impure thoughts; thoughts of suspicion and self-pity; thoughts of anger, hatred and violence; distorted thoughts; prideful thoughts; obsessive thoughts. Your head needs an infusion of divine glory.

David wrote in his most famous psalm, "You anoint my head with oil" (Psalm 23:5). Pouring oil on the head was a common Old Testament practice that symbolizes a significant New Testament truth—the anointing of the Spirit. The powerful presence of the Spirit in my life and in my mind brings spiritual victory, as David wrote in the same psalm, "You prepare a table before me *in the presence of my enemies.*"

And in Psalm 94:19 we read these lovely, liberating words: "When anxiety was great within me, your consolation brought joy to my soul." A struggle of life and death rages in my mind, and the anointing of God's presence restores my sanity. The mind that is set on the Spirit is life and peace.

This is precisely the theme of one of the best known passages in the New Testament on the subject of spiritual warfare, 2 Corinthians 10:3–5. "For though we live in the world, we do not wage war as the world does" (verse 3). In other words, what appears in the natural to be nothing more than a circumstantial problem may in fact have a spiritual cause.

The natural man does not understand the spiritual dimension and looks at life only through the eyes of his body. But the weapons of the Christian "are not the weapons of the world. On the contrary, they have divine power to demolish strongholds" (verse 4). Specifically, these are strongholds of the mind: arguments, pretensions, imaginations and every thought that is not taken captive to make it obedient to Christ. The mind is a battleground of spiritual strongholds and high places.

The longer I serve in ministry and the more I study spiritual warfare, the more I have become convinced that *our thoughts are often influenced by demons.* Not only do we need the helmet of salvation in the sense that our minds need to be saved from old patterns of thinking, but also for guarding our minds against the invasion of demonic influence. Let me explain *how* this happens.

How We Hear "Voices"

Our human nature has two principal aspects: physical and nonphysical. Genesis 2:7 records the creation of the first person: "The Lord God formed man from the dust of the ground [physical] and breathed into his nostrils the breath of life [nonphysical] . . . and man became a living being [that is, fully alive and human]." The physical aspect of our humanity operates through the senses of sight, hearing, taste, touch and smell. These make us conscious of the physical world around us.

The nonphysical side of our humanity may be further "divided" into soul and spirit (see Hebrews 4:12). The soul is each person's unique personality or self. The Greek word translated "soul" is *psyche,* from which we derive the English word *psychology.* Psychology, simply defined, is the study of the self as the fountainhead of human behavior. The soul may be further defined as mind (what we think), will (what we do) and emotions (what we feel). The mind, as I discussed earlier in this chapter, shapes our actions and feelings. The other nonphysical part, the spirit, is the human capacity for God and spiritual things. It is the "otherliness" of our humanity.

The body, then, is our world-side, the soul is our self-side and the spirit is our God-side. Humanity in its fullness is a unique balance and blend of world-consciousness, self-consciousness and God-consciousness.

I have developed a simple diagram to illustrate this.

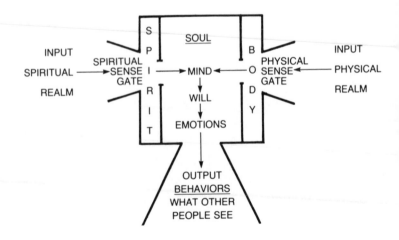

This diagram shows how the soul (mind, will, emotions) is influenced by "input" from the physical and spiritual dimensions. Once again, the mind is center stage, because it processes and stores information collected by our physical senses. What happens in our minds depends to a large degree on what we sense physically. If our eyes are blind and our ears deaf, then our minds will be correspondingly blank. People who are visually impaired, for example, rarely dream in color, because their eyes have never allowed that kind of information to enter the brain.

Most people do not realize, however, that the "sights and sounds" of the spiritual realm can penetrate our minds just as easily. Just as our minds are influenced by what our physical ears hear, our thoughts are similarly influenced by what our spiritual ears are hearing, often subliminally and unconsciously. This idea of *spiritual* seeing and hearing is, of course, a solidly biblical concept. In the opening chapters of Revelation, for example, Jesus challenged each of seven churches, "He who has an ear, let him hear what the Spirit says to the churches" (Revelation 2:7).

Another example is the story of Elisha and the siege of Dothan (2 Kings 6:8–22). To ease the fearfulness of his young assistant, Elisha prayed, "O Lord, open his eyes so he may see." At once the young man's eyes were opened and, to his astonishment, he beheld an incredible display of angelic power encircling and protecting them.

It is possible to see into the spiritual dimension. It may not always be easy, for now we see through a glass darkly (1 Corinthians 13:12). But occasionally the veil is lifted and we get a glimpse of true spiritual reality.

Christian believers are not the only ones, however, with a capacity for spiritual things. A person who has not been born again is not necessarily blind; deceived, yes, but not

dead to spirits and spirituality. Every human being, saved
or unsaved, has an intrinsic ability to "hear voices." Some
have referred to this as premonition or just ordinary intu-
ition. Whatever we call it, this human faculty for spirituality is very real and very dangerous: "The god of this age
has blinded the minds of unbelievers, so that they cannot
see the light of the gospel of the glory of Christ" (2 Corinthians 4:4). Unbelievers may have all kinds of spiritual
experiences, but they cannot see Christ because of the
spiritual power over their minds.

Kurt Koch, well-known worldwide as a lecturer on the
occult, is the author of the highly acclaimed book *Christian
Counseling and Occultism.* Regarding the power of compul-
sive thoughts and delusions, he writes,

> In the pastoral care of people subjected to occultism we
> find, besides the psychiatric phenomena, compulsive ideas
> [thoughts] like fear of mistakes, scruples, compulsions to
> make vows, to conversion, to confession, to reparation, to
> doubt and, above all, to blasphemy. . . . Dr. Lechler ad-
> mits, in the case of the blasphemous compulsion of an
> emotionally stable person, the further possibility of de-
> monic enslavement (p. 203).

Human spiritual potential is God-given, but when it is
at the mercy of the carnal nature, it is an open door for
demonic deception and oppression. Christians are different in that their ears have been opened to the right Spirit:
"My sheep listen to *my voice,*" Jesus affirmed. "I know
them" (John 10:27).

And yet Christians without discernment can be just as
readily influenced by "this present darkness." That
Christians can be controlled by demons is the thesis of

the comprehensive publication I mentioned earlier, *Demon Possession and the Christian: A New Perspective* by C. Fred Dickason, chairman of the theology department at Moody Bible Institute.

Satan's Influence on the Mind

Matthew 16 is probably the best example of biblical evidence of Satan's direct influence on the human mind. Jesus queried His disciples, "What are people saying about Me? What have you been hearing?" After a bit of discussion, Jesus turned to Peter and asked: "Who do you say I am?" Peter's famous reply was, "You are the Christ, the Son of the living God" (verse 16).

Listen to Jesus' commentary on Peter's profession: "This was not revealed to you by man, but by my Father in heaven" (verse 17). Jesus made it plain that Peter's thought, confessed openly by Peter's mouth, was not something originating in Peter's brain. Peter "heard a voice," the voice of the heavenly Father. It was not an audible voice, but was a voice spoken in Peter's *spiritual* ear, which caused an unexpected thought in his mind about the identity of Jesus. In the context of the diagram on page 128, spiritual input resulted in behavioral output.

There is something else here that is highly significant but easily overlooked. Jesus specifically identified the source of Peter's thought, but before that moment, *Peter was oblivious to the spiritual dynamics affecting his mind.* He was an unknowing recipient of divine revelation.

In this same chapter, Matthew 16, Peter's mind did a kind of spiritual reversal. When Jesus predicted His death, "Peter took him aside and began to rebuke him, 'Never, Lord!' " (verse 22). Peter was just expressing his concern, he thought, but Jesus again discerned the real source of Peter's "noble idea"—the devil himself. Jesus stunned His disciple with a terrible rebuke: "Out of my sight, Satan!" (verse 23). Again, *Peter was oblivious to the spiritual dynamics affecting his mind.* He was an unwitting recipient of spiritual deception.

This is only one of many examples in the Bible of how Satan bends the minds of unsuspecting people. His schemes are elusive and covert. His work is almost always impossible to identify, and he will give us every cause to believe that he has nothing to do with how we think, and thus how we feel and act.

Acts 5 records the tragic story of Ananias and Sapphira. The Peter of this event is markedly different from the earlier Peter of Matthew 16. His spiritual discernment has come a long way! Like Jesus, he is not fooled by the devil's methods. He blasts Ananias, "How is it that Satan has so filled your heart* that you have lied to the Holy Spirit? . . . What made you think of doing such a thing?" (verses 3–4). Judas was similarly prompted by the devil to betray Jesus (John 13:2). Neither of these men, I suspect, was fully aware of the power of demons to deceive him.

And listen to Paul's warning: "The Spirit clearly says that in later times some will abandon the faith and follow deceiving spirits and things taught by demons" (1 Timothy 4:1). The terrifying thing about this is that people who are in spiritual deception cannot recognize it.

---

*A strong case can be made that *heart* and *mind* are used interchangeably in the Bible. In our language, we distinguish between thoughts of the mind and feelings of the heart. This distinction is by no means clear in early Hebrew and later New Testament thought. An example is Proverbs 23:7: "For as he thinketh in his heart, so is he" (KJV).

I have never met anyone in religious deception who openly admitted, "I have considered the options, and this is my best choice. I have decided to follow deceiving spirits." Deception is not like buying groceries. It is more like eating cheese from a rat trap. Those who deny the influence of the trap have no inkling that they are in denial, and therein lies its power and control. In another place Paul wrote, "I am afraid that just as Eve was deceived by the serpent's cunning, *your minds may somehow be led astray from your sincere and pure devotion to Christ*" (2 Corinthians 11:3).

Most of our thoughts are self-initiated. I think most of my own thoughts. But demonic promptings always remain a real and present possibility. The battle rages for our minds. Be totally changed, then, by the renewing of your minds, bringing every thought into captivity to the obedience of Christ. Put on the helmet of salvation. "Whatever is true, whatever is noble, whatever is right, whatever is pure, whatever is lovely, whatever is admirable—if anything is excellent or praiseworthy— think about such things" (Philippians 4:8). "Above all else, guard your heart, for it is the wellspring of life" (Proverbs 4:23).

Discerning the Spirits

How can I guard my thoughts? How can I know where my thoughts are coming from? Discernment is both a gift and a learned skill.

The gift. Paul includes "the ability to distinguish between spirits" in his list of the nine supernatural manifestations of the Holy Spirit in 1 Corinthians 12 (see verse 10). There are three kinds of spirits: evil spirits, human spirits and heavenly spirits, including angels and the Spirit of God. The discerning of spirits is the ability to identify the kind of spirit that is the driving force behind a particular event, circumstance or thought. If it is determined that the spirit is an evil one, the discerning of spirits operating with precision can also identify the specific kind of evil spirit.

The skill. Discernment is also a learned skill. The writer of Hebrews describes mature Christians as those "who by constant use have trained themselves to distinguish good from evil" (Hebrews 5:14). Spiritual maturity and wise perception do not develop overnight. There is no getting around it. Sometimes we just have to learn the hard way, chopping a path through the jungle of experience. The only way to get older and wiser is to get older—and wiser!

Thus, remaining teachable and listening to others is paramount, especially when you are young. Paul wrote to the very immature Corinthians, "Even though you have ten thousand guardians in Christ, you do not have many fathers" (1 Corinthians 4:15). Anyone in the church pew will give you advice, and if you ask enough of the "ten thousand" you will always find someone who will tell you what you want to hear.

There are, however, very few spiritual fathers, mature Christians adequately skilled in the Word and in the experiences of life, people who can give you real help. And spiritual fathers are willing to make the personal sacrifice necessary to walk you through your problems, unlike the man on the street who will give you free advice about anything.

Youth must listen to age. Immaturity must submit itself to maturity (1 Peter 5:5–6) and all of us need to submit to one another (Ephesians 5:21). Every word, every thought should be tested by two or three witnesses. We guard our minds by submitting our thoughts to one another.

Lastly, we sharpen our discernment skills through the regular practice of the spiritual disciplines. Prayer, fasting, worship and Bible reading are exercises that strengthen and develop our spiritual senses. *The Celebration of Discipline* by Richard Foster is an excellent guide to understanding these fundamental regimens of the Christian life.* Discipline is a price we must pay for the fine-tuning of our spiritual sensitivity. We must watch carefully and pray fervently. Our adversary the devil prowls about, looking for unsuspecting, undiscerning victims. But as we take up the helmet of salvation and stand in right relationship with God we will find that Satan's tricks become more obvious and readily combated.

A prayer for putting on the helmet of salvation: Heavenly Father, forgive me for my wandering thoughts and undisciplined thinking. I realize that I have not been guarding my heart, and I have allowed wrong thoughts to influence and even control me. I resist those thoughts in the name of Jesus, and in the power of His might I cast down every stronghold of wrong thinking: imaginations, pride, self-pity, anger, deceit. Give me a clear head. Grant me spiritual discernment to recognize the origin of my thoughts. I am committing myself to thinking right and thinking

---

* This book was quite helpful to me personally, and I have used it as a "textbook" for an adult Bible class on the disciplines of the Christian life. Some of Foster's critics, however, have concerns about his chapter on meditation, particularly the suggestion to imagine your spiritual body leaving your physical body (p. 27). This chapter, I think, should be read with caution.

straight. Deliver me from every distortion and misunderstanding. And Lord, give me the strength to refrain from speaking out my thoughts unless I am certain that what I say will bring honor to You and life to others. I pray this in Jesus' mighty name, Amen.

Part III
The Weapons of Our Warfare

Overcoming the Dominion of Darkness

10

The Power of the Spirit

"God anointed Jesus of Nazareth with the Holy Spirit
and power."   Acts 10:38
"But you will receive power when the Holy Spirit
comes on you."   Acts 1:8

You cannot argue with a demon. Human strength is completely inadequate in spiritual warfare, and the only power that will prevail over the spirit of darkness is the Spirit of God; spirit must be confronted by Spirit. What happened to Jesus in this regard should happen to us. The book of Acts is the story of the people of God receiving what Jesus received—the Spirit—in order to do what Jesus did— prevail in Kingdom ministry.

The One baptized in the Spirit at the Jordan River becomes the One who baptizes in the Spirit. Jesus preached the Kingdom, did Kingdom works and prevailed over the ancient enemy. The secret of His power was the outpouring of the Holy Spirit. This is a crucial point: *The power of the Kingdom of God is the power of the Spirit, and the power of the Spirit is the only way that the Kingdom of God will prevail over the kingdom of darkness.*

Jesus and the Spirit: The Christ

The Kingdom ministry in the life of Christ was powered by the Holy Spirit. This theological concept is clearly pre-

139

sented in Luke's Gospel. As prolific writer and theologian Michael Green wrote in *I Believe in the Holy Spirit*, "Luke persistently links the coming of the messianic age with the gift of the Spirit" (p. 38).

Jesus began His public ministry by reading aloud the declaration in Isaiah, "The Spirit of the Lord is on me, because he has anointed me . . . " (Luke 4:18). Matthew highlighted the connection between Jesus and Isaiah's prophecies, "This was to fulfill what was spoken . . . : 'Here is my servant whom I have chosen, the one I love, in whom I delight; I will put my Spirit *on* him' " (Matthew 12:17–18; see also Isaiah 42:1–4). And in Acts 10:38 we read that "God anointed Jesus of Nazareth with the Holy Spirit and power, and how he went around doing good and healing all who were under the power of the devil."

The anointing of the Spirit takes us back to the Old Testament practice of anointing with oil in which Israel's chosen leaders were authorized to represent Jehovah on the earth. Jesus is the consummate prophet, priest and king, authorized not by oil, but by the Spirit, to reestablish the Kingdom of God and to overcome the dominion of darkness. Jesus was "the Christ," the anointed One, anointed by the Spirit to do the work of the Kingdom, to restore the Dominion Commission of Genesis 1:26.

What happened to Jesus when He was baptized in the Spirit? At least four things.

First, there was a release of Kingdom power. When Jesus was authorized by the Spirit to do the work of the Father, the government of God was placed on His shoulder and demonstrable power was released in His life. As at Pentecost, the Spirit baptism of Jesus was accompanied *and followed* by signs, wonders and spiritual giftings.

Second, the Spirit brought on Jesus an affirmation of Sonship and mission. When Jesus was baptized, the heavens were opened, and a voice said, "You are my Son, whom I love; with you I am well pleased" (Luke 3:22). This was no doubt a reference to the messianic promise of Psalm 2:7: "I will proclaim the decree of the Lord: He said to me, 'You are my Son; today I have become your Father.' "

Jesus was the Son forever (John 1:1), while the Incarnation—union of deity with humanity—occurred at the moment of His conception in Mary's womb. Jesus knew something of His destiny at the age of twelve, but the full consciousness of His identity, His mission and certainly the power to fulfill that mission did not occur until His baptism in the Jordan and in the Spirit. The gift of the Spirit descending on Jesus at His baptism was to be understood as a sign of His "official" adoption as Son.

In *Jesus and the Spirit* British theologian James Dunn writes, "Out of this confidence that he stood in a specially intimate relation with God arose Jesus' sense of mission. Sonship meant to Jesus not a dignity to be claimed, but a responsibility to be fulfilled" (p. 39). The coming of the Spirit on Jesus was an affirmation of His Sonship and mission.

Third, the Spirit baptism of Jesus led almost immediately to spiritual warfare. His hair still wet from the Jordan, Jesus was whisked by the Spirit into the wilderness to confront the serpent. The coming of the Spirit upon Jesus brought Kingdom authority, and an immediate clash of the Kingdom of light and the dominion of darkness. Without the coming of the Spirit, this would never have occurred. Satan raises his ugly head only when his dominion is seriously challenged, and his authority is decisively contested when the Holy Spirit is present in power.

Fourth, the coming of the Spirit on Jesus initiated effective ministry. There is no reference in the Scriptures to any public ministry in the life of Christ prior to His baptism in the Spirit. With the exception of the events attending His birth and the story of the boy Jesus in the Temple, the New Testament is strangely silent about His child-hood years. Only Matthew and Luke mention His birth, but all four Gospels give careful attention to His baptism. The baptism of Christ is the crucial starting point for His public ministry and, for that matter, all of the New Tes-tament that follows.

It is significant that the Gospel writers focus almost ex-clusively on the ministry words and works of Jesus *after* He received the Spirit. The coming of the Spirit upon Jesus resulted in Kingdom authority, by which Jesus overcame the devil and began effective public ministry. Effective public ministry means that the Kingdom of Christ is over-coming the dominion of darkness.

Christians and the Spirit: Anointed Ones

The Spirit baptism of Jesus was intended to be a model experience for every Christian. It was a necessary empow-ering to fulfill the Dominion Commission. "Christ-ians" are "anointed ones" ("little Christs"), just as Jesus was the Anointed One, the Christ. Our natures differ. Jesus was God incarnate, but the Spirit who came upon Him is the same Spirit in whom He baptizes believers to be His wit-nesses and to do His work.

Thomas Smail wrote in *Reflected Glory*, "In both Christ and us the Spirit is working with the stuff of our common humanity; because He is man and we are men, it becomes possible and credible that what the Spirit did in Him, He should be able to do again in us" (p. 63). We have examined what the Spirit did in Jesus. Let's see what happens when the Spirit comes on us.

First, He releases Kingdom authority and power in us. Jesus has transferred His authority to the Church. The Great Commission to go into all the world is entirely dependent on the premise that appears in the preceding verse: "All authority in heaven and on earth has been given to me. Therefore go . . . " (Matthew 28:18–19). Jesus is commissioning us to make disciples in the context of the restoration of God's authority in a godless and demonized world. It is clear in the other Great Commission accounts in Luke, Acts and Mark that the power of which Jesus speaks— authority in heaven and in earth—is none other than the Pentecostal outpouring of the Holy Spirit.

In Luke's account of the Great Commission, both in his Gospel and in Acts, Jesus expects His disciples to wait in Jerusalem for the coming of the Spirit's power (Luke 24:48– 49; Acts 1:8). And Mark predicts powerful signs and wonders will follow those who respond in faith to the Great Commission (Mark 16:15–18). Even though the textual validity of this last chapter in Mark is disputed, it certainly demonstrates the belief of the early Church: To be empowered by the same Spirit that came upon Jesus is to do the works of power Jesus did.

Second, when the Holy Spirit comes upon Christians there is a special affirmation of Sonship and mission. When Jesus received the Spirit, a voice from heaven spoke proclaiming His unique relationship with the heavenly Father, and what that union meant in terms of God's mission for His life.

Something very similar occurs when the Spirit comes upon the believer. "For you did not receive a spirit that makes you a slave again to fear, *but you received the Spirit of sonship*. And by him we cry, 'Abba, Father.' The Spirit himself testifies with our spirit *that we are God's children"* (Romans 8:15–16). Those who have been Spirit-baptized have a deep and certain consciousness of their union with God, and their accompanying destiny: the Kingdom Commission. Just look what happened to the disciples when the Spirit came at Pentecost!

Third, Holy Spirit baptism is a declaration of war. Immediately after His baptism, Jesus was led by the Spirit into the desert to confront the ancient serpent in a kind of replay of Eden. The setting and players were different, but the devil's story line was the same. Jesus did not succumb, however, showing us that the empowering of the Spirit also enables the believer to be victorious in the conflict of the kingdoms, to rule and reign with Christ over the powers of darkness. Kingdom authority is not possible without the Spirit's power.

In a kind of pre-Pentecost training exercise, Jesus commissioned seventy of His disciples to announce the Kingdom and to heal the sick. When they returned and recounted the dramatic signs that accompanied their ministry, Jesus relayed a moment of revelation. He had seen Satan fall from heaven like a bolt of lightning, to which He added this significant comment: "I have given you authority to tread upon serpents and scorpions, and over all the power of the enemy" (Luke 10:19, NAS).

We find this same theme in Ephesians 1:18–19, where Paul prays for his followers to see the light, that the eyes of their hearts may be enlightened in order to know "the incomparably great power for us who believe." It is that power of the Spirit that raised Christ from the dead (see Romans 8:11). And that same power established Him as the Head of the Church over all "rule and authority, power and dominion . . . not only in the present age but also in the one to come" (Ephesians 1:21).

The theme of Ephesians is the Church and her heavenly warfare (see Ephesians 6:10–18), and, like Jesus, believers must be empowered by the Spirit to triumph over Satan. The fire of hell can be overcome only by the fire of the Spirit.

Fourth, when the Spirit comes upon Christians, He launches the Church, like Jesus, into powerful public ministry. For Jesus, public ministry was not limited to speaking out on religious or social issues. When the Spirit came on Jesus, signs of the Kingdom followed. He preached great messages, but miracles confirmed the word. The same thing happened when the Spirit came upon the Church in the book of Acts. The power of the Spirit transformed a small, reclusive band of quivering disciples into a spiritual army that turned the world upside-down.*

The Spirit Within and Upon

It is important to make a distinction between the two principal aspects of the work of the Spirit. On the one hand, the New Testament clearly teaches the concept of the Spirit dwelling *within* the believer. This aspect of the Spirit's work produces the *fruits* listed in Galatians 5:22–23 (love, joy, peace, longsuffering, etc.). On the other hand, the Spirit's work, which I have been developing in this chapter, involves the release of *Kingdom power and ministry gifts upon* the believer. The Spirit *within* develops our char-

---

* Some believe that the supernatural gifts of the Spirit "died out" with the apostles. I discuss this at length in my first book, *And Signs Shall Follow: A Look at the Most Misunderstood Points of Charismatic Teaching.*

acter. The Spirit *upon* releases ministry. I diagram it this way:

Spirit Within	⟶	Fruit	⟶	Maturity
Spirit Upon	⟶	Gifts	⟶	Ministry

Jesus is our prototype. He was conceived by the Holy Spirit (born of the Spirit, we could say), God made flesh. Jesus is a kind of firstfruits of the born-again Christian. Like Jesus, we become partakers of the divine nature through spiritual birth (see 1 Peter 1:4). The difference, of course, is that Jesus had no sin nature. He was conceived and birthed by the Spirit, not born again. As a consequence of the nature and Spirit of God *within* Him, Jesus grew in wisdom and in favor with God and man (Luke 2:52), but this alone was not enough to qualify Him for leadership. Nor did it prepare Him for Kingdom ministry and spiritual warfare.

It was not until the Holy Spirit came *upon* Jesus that He began His power ministry. He affirmed His calling on the basis of the Spirit *upon* Him, not His wonderful, godly life (the Spirit *within* Him).

In *Secret Power* the great evangelist D. L. Moody once wrote,

> The Holy Spirit dwelling in us, is one thing: I think this is clearly brought out in Scripture; and the Holy Spirit upon us for service is another thing. . . . Every believer has the Holy Ghost dwelling in him. He may be quenching the Spirit of God, and he may not glorify God as he should, but if he is a believer on the Lord Jesus Christ, the Holy Ghost dwells in him. But . . . though Christian men and women have the Holy Spirit dwelling in them, yet He is not dwelling within them in power; in other words, God

has a great many sons and daughters without power. . . .
Then, the Holy Spirit in us is one thing, and the Holy Spirit
on us is another (pp. 33–48).

Christians today commonly fail to make this distinction.
On the one hand some believe we receive all of the Spirit
at the moment of salvation. This view generally overlooks
the need for power ministry as exemplified by Jesus and
the early Church. It also explains how Christians can be
mature, yet seem to lack spiritual power and perception.

On the other hand, I have heard people say, "I need the
outpouring of the Spirit's power so I can live a more con-
sistent Christian life." As I understand the Bible, the Pentecostal experience of the Holy Spirit does not make a
person a better Christian. Even Jesus, when He received
the Spirit, did not become "better" in the quality of His
life. Paul affirms this same principle in his first letter to the
Corinthians, who excelled in the power gifts but lacked
basic Christian virtues. This explains how Christians can
be so gifted and yet immature at the same time.

Godliness is not born in a charismatic moment. It results
from years of disciplined obedience to the Scriptures. Jesus submitted to the Father and learned the Scriptures for
thirty years. Only then was He anointed for ministry. The
outpouring of the Spirit on Jesus authorized and empowered Him to do the works of the Kingdom. Now Jesus
baptizes us in the same Spirit, authorizing and empowering us to do the work of the Kingdom.

The Spirit and the Spiritual Realm

When the Spirit comes in power, He opens the door to
the spiritual realm. When the Spirit came upon Jesus,

"heaven was opened" (Luke 3:21). Not surprisingly, we see a parallel in the book of Acts. On the Day of Pentecost, the heavens were opened again. The text of Peter's Pentecost sermon was this well-known passage from Joel's prophecy:

> "In the last days, God says, I will pour out my Spirit on all people. [Notice the results:] Your sons and daughters *will prophesy,* your young men will *see visions,* your old men will *dream dreams.* . . . I will pour out my Spirit in those days, and they will *prophesy.*"
>
> Acts 2:17–18

The prophets of old were called "seers," because they could see into the invisible, spiritual realm. This is precisely what happens when the Holy Spirit comes upon believers. I refer again to the diagram in chapter 9, to which I have added the entrance of the Spirit's power.

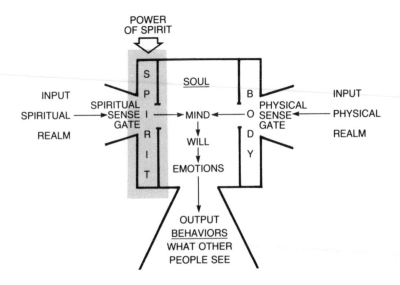

The Spirit lifts the curtain on the stage of the spiritual dimension and gives us the power to overcome the spirits of darkness. Our knowledge and prophecy are partial (1 Corinthians 13:9). We do not "see" the whole picture, but if the Spirit does not open up the heavens, we will not see anything at all.

This may have been Paul's reason for writing, "Eagerly desire spiritual gifts, *especially the gift of prophecy*" (1 Corinthians 14:1). Why? Because prophecy penetrates the invisible spiritual dimension: "The secrets of [a person's] heart will be laid bare. So he will fall down and worship God, exclaiming, 'God is really among you!' " (1 Corinthians 14:25). Prophecy "sees" and discerns, and the coming of the Spirit makes that happen.

Prophecy, then, is an exemplary spiritual gift. All the supernatural gifts, however, are significant because they reach beyond what is natural and visible. The spiritual gifts are not just charismatic entertainment. They are expressions of the only kind of power capable of overcoming the dominion of darkness. If they were necessary in the life of Jesus and the early Church, they are essential in the life of the believer today.*

---

* The purpose of this book is not to discuss each of the spiritual gifts and their uses in the Church. I highly recommend two books: *Your Spiritual Gifts Can Help Your Church Grow* by Peter Wagner on spiritual gift discovery, and *Spiritual Gifts in the Local Church* by David Pytches on understanding and using the power gifts.

11
The Sword of the Spirit

Take . . . the sword of the Spirit, which is the word of
God.   Ephesians 6:17

I learned a crucial lesson about spiritual warfare the hard
way. The year 1987 was the most difficult of my life. The
final two months of the year were horrible, and the last
week was the worst. After a long battle with cancer, our
church's visitation pastor, Warren Hill, died late in the
evening on the last Sunday of 1987. His daughter called
me early Monday morning.

Within an hour I picked up the phone again. This time
my secretary was calling. In a subdued voice she told me
that our receptionist, Bobbi Jo, and her husband, Bob, coming home from a holiday vacation, were in a terrible automobile accident in New Mexico. Bob did not make it. I offi-
ciated back-to-back funerals the last two days of December.

The thing that helped me hang on the most was the
sword of the Spirit. Were it not for the Word of God coming alive I doubt I could have made it. Let me show you
what I mean.

At that time most of our congregation did not know I
was facing a health crisis myself. During the previous
month, I had developed a heart problem of unknown
cause—at the ripe old age of 38. I was taking a strong

arrhythmia medication, which has since been severely restricted in its applications by the FDA. I will never forget asking the pharmacist about the side effects of the medicine. Staring at the lengthy statement of applications and limitations, he asked me, "Were you on anything else before taking this?"

"No," I replied apprehensively. "Well," he said, still scrutinizing the document, "this seems to be for people when other medication does not work." You can imagine what that did for me.

Things had begun to unravel a few weeks before. I staggered home one Sunday evening, characteristically exhausted after our four-service Sunday. As I lay in bed, I became aware of a strange sensation in my chest. I checked my pulse. My heart was palpitating erratically, missing a beat every few seconds.

In a mild panic, I called the emergency room at the local hospital. They reassured me that my problem as I described it was fairly common, but I had difficulty believing them. I was in good aerobic condition, and I never had a trace of a heart problem.

The next morning I scheduled an appointment with our family doctor. When I saw him at the end of the day, he arranged a special appointment for me to see a cardiologist immediately. I was given a battery of tests, among them an overnight heart monitor. This last procedure showed that I had six or seven "misfires" every minute, or more than 9000 irregular beats in a twenty-four-hour period.

The doctor was uncertain of my condition, and I was very frightened. With some of the test results still pending, I decided to get away for a few days to rest and to seek the Lord. To add to my discouragement, my lifetime friend, a radiologist physician, was undergoing surgery the same weekend—in an attempt to arrest his recently discovered leukemia.

When my wife and I returned on Sunday afternoon, my son greeted me with more bad news. That same morning, our associate pastor's wife was in a serious auto accident on the way home from church. It was a miracle that she survived the crash with only minor injuries. She came within inches of death when her little car was struck in the intersection. And the other vehicle was being driven by someone else from our church!

Her husband, Bob, was preaching at the time, and one of our ushers interrupted his sermon to give him the news. After courageously finishing his message, he rushed to the hospital to see his wife.

I felt helpless in the hurricane of trouble. The next day I was scheduled to return to the cardiologist for more test results, so I spent the early morning seeking God. You tend to do that when life is falling apart.

I will never forget the flash of the sword of the Spirit—how God spoke to me, and what He said. My Bible literally fell open to Psalm 118 and these verses stood out—seemingly written just for me:

> I will not die but live, and will proclaim what the Lord has done. The Lord has chastened me severely, but he has not given me over to death.   verses 17–18

My personal journal for that day reads,

> God gives me this word: Psalm 118:17–18, at 9 A.M. Dr. appointment at 11. The EKG, X rays, and doctor's prognosis all positive. I can even exercise! (In moderation of course, no soccer for a while.) Why all the terrible physical

feelings? Doctor does not know. I think nerves. I think the whole thing is stress—with no little mixture of spiritual conflict. I have not been good at standing—I have been very fearful, but God has been faithful.

That was two years ago as of this writing. My heart problem has virtually disappeared, and I am no longer taking any medication. Our church weathered the many crises, and we learned a great deal about wrestling with the devil. God gave me a liberating, living word, a "sword of the Spirit," to cut through the cloud of emotional and spiritual darkness. Let's see how to brandish that sword when the attacks of the enemy and life's tragedies seem to be closing in.

Rhema: The Spoken, Living Word

One Greek term for "word" is *rhema* (plural *rhemata*), which refers to a spoken, living word. Another term, *logos,* is also translated "word," but *logos* has a broader meaning in the sense of truth, ideas, doctrines. Admittedly, *logos* and *rhema* are often used interchangeably in the New Testament, but *rhema* denotes a particular statement.

According to *A Manual Greek Lexicon of the New Testament* a *rhema* is a precise spoken word for a specific situation in your life. It is the Bible in its most personal kind of application. The Word of God made alive by the Holy Spirit has spiritual power. Unlike the armor of God for protection and defense, the sword of the Spirit is an offensive weapon for assaulting the strongholds of the enemy.

"For a sword, take that which the Spirit gives you—the words that come from God" (Ephesians 6:17, NEB). Spiritual victory is not attained by human strength, not even by the power of personal confession. It is by the Spirit of God undergirding the words we speak. Jesus declared, "The Spirit gives life; the flesh counts for nothing. The words [*rhemata*] I have spoken to you are spirit and they are life" (John 6:63).

The crucial lesson, one we have raised repeatedly in this book, is that you cannot counteract spiritual forces with human strength. For the Christian, the formula for victorious living includes both the Word and the Spirit. Carefully stated doctrines are not enough to overcome the enemy. Even the demons believe what we believe (James 2:19). In fact, Satan's "doctrinal statement" is undoubtedly more accurate and precisely defined than the best systematic theology textbook money can buy.

The devil is not threatened by correct doctrine alone, but he flees from the believer who obeys God's Word and is strong in the Spirit. The apostle Paul boasted, "My message and my preaching were not with wise and persuasive words, but with *a demonstration of the Spirit's power*" (1 Corinthians 2:4).

Even Jesus withstood Satan by the Word and the Spirit. Look up the temptation passages in a red-letter Bible, which highlights the words of Jesus (Matthew 4:1–11 and Luke 4:1–13). Notice how Jesus did not dialogue with the devil? Nor did He rely on superior intellect or even His deity. And unlike so many unequipped Christians, Jesus was not desperately flipping through His concordance for an emergency Bible verse either. Instead, He was "full of the Holy Spirit" (Luke 4:1). Satan fled, because Jesus spoke God's Word, a timely word and an anointed word, a *rhema*.

Imagine visiting a doctor for the first time. During the appointment you discover you are his first official patient. New on the job, he is a bit tentative in his diagnosis of

your problem. Reaching for his fresh pharmaceutical sam-
ples, he prescribes a different pill each day for the next
week. Would you ever return to his office? Would you
report him for malpractice?

Certain ailments require a precise diagnosis, followed
by a specific prescription. I don't take an antibiotic for a
headache, or chemotherapy for a dislocated shoulder.
Christian growth and spiritual warfare are no different. I
need specific and relevant words from God so I am able to
deal with my problems and counter the equally specific
schemes of the dominion of darkness.

If you are facing a particularly difficult situation, or trying to overcome a temptation or break a habit, you need a
rhema, a special power word from the Spirit of God. Just
reading the Bible or listening to Christian music will not
resolve long-term issues. Study the Bible with a purpose.
Let the Holy Spirit guide you as you select three or four
references that apply specifically to your problem.

Christian psychologist and author Norman Wright rec-
ommends a "stop card" to confront your emotions and
"just say no." On a 3 × 5 card, write a spiritual prescription—a Bible verse or statement of truth that applies directly to your problem. Carry it with you. When the
problem flares up or when the devil comes against you
and you feel your emotional self-control slipping, read the
card aloud.

I have employed this strategy with great success during
the most troubling times in my life. I write down what
God has spoken to my heart when I am in a more stable,
spiritual frame of mind, like during prayer and fasting, or
in church. Then during life's darker moments I read aloud
what God has given me in the light. It works. When Jesus

is Lord of my thoughts, I am able to control myself and
bind the devil.

How to Receive a *Rhema*

The key is the *rhema*. I don't want to borrow a Bible
verse that worked for someone else. I must depend on the
"sword of the Spirit, which is the *rhema* of God." If you
need a living word, then put this book down now. Spend
some time alone with God and ask for specific divine guidance in your situation.

James puts it this way: "Consider it pure joy, my
brothers, whenever you face trials of many kinds. . . . If
any of you lacks wisdom, he should ask God" (James
1:2, 5). How to get direction from God (James 1:5–8) is
sandwiched between teaching on trials (James 1:1--4) and
temptations (James 1:12–15). In other words, James is ed-
ucating us how to receive specific guidance from God
when we really need help. God *will* give you wisdom,
and He won't make you feel guilty about talking with
Him honestly about your problems. He really wants to
help you.

For James, "wisdom" is practical, not theoretical religious concepts. We frequently misconceive God's wisdom
as spiritual ideas and principles, and our favorite question
in life is "Why?" But James 1 is not a treatise on the cause
of trouble, the *why*. It is a revelation of *how* to be spiritually
successful regardless of the cause of the trial or its ultimate
outcome.

When you ask "Why?" as in, "Why did this happen to
me?," you will usually come up with an answer that
does not help you through the trouble. Job had as much
trouble as anyone could imagine. He did not need an ex-

planation. His friends tried that approach. Job needed God.

When wrestling with the devil, a better question than "Why?" is *"How?"* How do I get out of this mess? Even in the Old Testament, the idea of wisdom is pragmatic. The Hebrew term translated "wisdom" actually refers to the practical skill of a craftsman, not the intellectual wisdom of a scholar. God's wisdom is revealed in His deeds and acts, not in His intellect alone.

It is not just what we think intellectually during a spiritual battle that counts, it is what we do. Concluding the Sermon on the Mount, Jesus told a parable of two men. One built his house on the sand, the other on the rock. It was the latter whose house withstood the ravages of the storm. And yet the one who built his house on the sand was hardly ignorant! He heard the Word, and perhaps he even understood. But he did not respond to what he heard. Picking up this same theme, James writes, "Do not merely listen to the word, and so deceive yourselves. *Do what it says*" (James 1:22).

God's wisdom works. When the devil tries to crowd into your life, ask God for wisdom. You can expect a *rhema*. This is the message of Revelation 12:10–11 as well: "Now have come the salvation and the power and the kingdom of our God, and the authority of his Christ. For the accuser of our brothers, who accuses them before our God day and night, has been hurled down. They overcame him by the blood of the Lamb. . . ." This is our eternal standing with God based on the finished work of Christ and the blood of the everlasting covenant.

They also overcame him "by the word of their testimony." *Logos* is used here, not *rhema*, but the idea of a living, relevant word is clearly implied. The saints overcame the dominion of darkness by the Word of God made real in their own lives—"the *word of their testimony*." What I learn from others will stir my faith. What I learn for myself in the crucible of personal experience will change me forever.

John put it this way: "For everyone born of God overcomes the world" (1 John 5:4). Whatever God does will remain: " 'Once more I will shake not only the earth but also the heavens' . . . so that what cannot be shaken may remain" (Hebrews 12:26–27).

Two years ago God gave me a *rhema*: "You will not die, but live." I have been severely tested and shaken, but His Word has sustained me. And as I continue to depend on the sword of the Spirit, this will remain the word of my testimony.

12
Binding and Loosing

"Whatever you bind on earth will be bound in heaven, and whatever you loose on earth will be loosed in heaven." Matthew 18:18

Our family dinner was about to begin. I asked our four-year-old son to thank God for the food. As he muttered some disconnected words about Jesus and dinner, I opened one eye and caught him contorting his face in a particularly religious fashion. I wanted to tell him, "You don't have to make funny faces to get God to listen to your prayers." And then it hit me. He was innocently mimicking his parents! I wanted to repent!

When I first witnessed power ministry, I prayed the way I heard others pray. Like the sons of Sceva (Acts 19:13–20), I rebuked demons the way I heard others rebuke them. I was even careful about my inflection. After all, if you are binding the devil, you have to do it with a voice that sounds authoritative. Or so I thought.

"*I bind you, devil!*" When you hear people say this, do you know what they mean? Do *they* know what they mean? I get the impression that for many believers, binding and loosing is a kind of Christian abracadabra—a phrase that somehow sends a rebuking bolt at the devil. For others, it is empty charismatic chatter—such as when

I'm turning steaks on the grill and the direction of the breeze shifts slightly. Reacting to the smoke in my eyes, I yell out, "I bind you, smoke!" My friends around me laugh, and one of them blurts out, "Praise the Lord!" One approach sincere, one in jest, but both ineffective.

Confronting demons is a grave business and, at times, highly complex. Binding and loosing is not spiritual magic. It has to do with the authority of the Christian in spiritual warfare, and there are often many factors involved. Simply defined, binding and loosing is a confident assurance and confession of God's order and government over against the disorder of a sin-cursed, demonized world. But there is also much more.

Binding, Loosing and the Great Commission

In what I call the Great Recommission, Jesus announced that He had been given *all* authority *in heaven and on the earth* (Matthew 28:18). Notice the parallel with our opening verse: "Whatever you bind *on earth* will be bound *in heaven*, and whatever you loose *on earth* will be loosed *in heaven*" (Matthew 18:18). Jesus was transferring and imparting His authority to the believer. When we pray like this, "Your kingdom come. Your will be done, on earth as it is in heaven," we are releasing the authority of Christ. Christians have the right and the responsibility to pray for change whenever anything is not under the Lordship of Christ.

Jesus came into the world as a firstfruits of God's purpose for His new humanity. The Spirit of the Lord was *upon* Him. He was authorized to "proclaim freedom for the prisoners . . . to release the oppressed, to proclaim the year of the Lord's favor" (Luke 4:18–19). As Jesus lived it, this was not a reference to political or social liberation.

The world's problems have never been primarily political or social, but spiritual, and this was the thrust of Jesus' ministry as He fulfilled the prophecy of Isaiah 61. "To release the oppressed" meant casting out the evil spirits that were holding people captive. It is striking that the first miracle recorded by Luke, immediately after Jesus' messianic declaration in Nazareth, was an exorcism (Luke 4:31–37).

Even John the Baptist, expecting a Messiah who would bring political and social reform, stumbled over Jesus' ministry. John's faith was wavering in a prison of despair: " 'Are you the one who was to come, or should we expect someone else?' Jesus replied, 'Go back and report to John what you hear and see: The blind receive sight, the lame walk, those who have leprosy are cured, the deaf hear, the dead are raised, and the good news is preached to the poor' " (Matthew 11:3–6). Jesus was a great social reformer, but He taught that permanent changes in people and society must begin in the spiritual realm.

Binding, Loosing and the Finished Work of Christ

Quoting Psalm 68:18, the apostle Paul declares that the risen Christ "led captivity captive" (Ephesians 4:8, KJV). The classic Bible expositor Matthew Henry wrote of this verse, "He conquered those who conquered us." Jesus is Lord, seated at the right hand of the throne of God, "far above all rule and authority, power and dominion, and every title that can be given, not only in the present age [on the earth] but also in the one to come [in heaven]" (Ephesians 1:21). God has placed all things under His feet, and Christ has transferred His authority to us to represent Him on the earth.

On the bedrock of His finished work and limitless spiritual authority, Jesus *will* build His Church. It was God's eternal purpose "that now [in this age, on the earth], *through the church*, [God's] manifold wisdom . . . should be made known to the rulers and authorities in the heavenly realms" (Ephesians 3:10). In anticipation of His complete victory, Jesus proclaimed that the gates of Hades will not prevail or stand against the Church (Matthew 16:18).

The gates of ancient cities were entrance points into the heart and life of the people who lived there. It was also common for the city fathers to conduct business and pass laws at the gates. Gates, then, took on a kind of symbolic significance so that the "gates of hell" are to be understood as the authority and counsels of the dominion of darkness. In other words, the purposes of God will prevail over the purposes of the devil, and God will fulfill His plan through the Church.

In this context, Jesus also promised, "I will give you the keys of the kingdom of heaven; whatever you bind on earth will be bound in heaven, and whatever you loose on earth will be loosed in heaven" (Matthew 16:19).

Binding and Loosing in Spiritual Warfare

The use of the phrase *binding and loosing* did not, in fact, originate with Jesus. It was a frequent expression of first century Jewish rabbinical dialect. According to Alexander

Bruce in *The Expositor's Greek New Testament* to bind and loose (Greek: *deo* and *luo*) meant simply "to prohibit and to permit," that is, to establish rules (Vol. 1, p. 225). The Jewish religious authorities at the time of Christ retained the right to establish guidelines for, or keys to, religious practice and social interaction.*

But *deo* (to bind, tie) also expresses supernatural control. In Luke 13:15–16, Jesus rebuked a Jewish leader,

> "You hypocrites! Doesn't each of you on the Sabbath untie [Greek: *luo*, loose] his ox or donkey from the stall and lead it out to give it water? Then should not this woman, a daughter of Abraham, whom Satan has kept bound [Greek: *deo*, bind] for eighteen long years, be set free [Greek: *luo*, loose] on the Sabbath day from what bound her?"

Binding and loosing is an activity of spiritual warfare. Satan himself will be bound (Greek: *deo*) with a great chain (Revelation 20:1–2), and even the conservative *Dictionary of New Testament Theology* admits cautiously that

> the idea of binding may also refer back to the picture of the binding of the strong man (that is, Satan) who must first be bound (the same verb, *deo*) before his goods (that is, those enthralled by him) may be plundered (Matt. 12:29, parallel Mk. 3:27; see also Lk. 11:21 which does not use [the same Greek] word). Thus Peter would be promised the power that Christ had to bind the powers of evil and to liberate men, and this would hold good not only on earth, but also in heaven (Vol. 2, p. 733).

* The Greek terms *deo* and *luo* are translations of the Hebrew *asar* and *hittir*. See Colin Brown, ed., *Dictionary of New Testament Theology*, Vol. 2, p. 732.

Binding and Loosing and God's Will

In chapter 4, I discussed the plural "you" used through-out the New Testament. Matthew 16:18 is an exception, where Jesus is speaking directly to Peter about the gates of Hades. In this sense, every individual believer has the right and responsibility to resist the devil. You, individu-ally, will be singled out and challenged by spirits of dark-ness and you, individually, must resist temptation, restrain yourself and stand your ground.

The same command to bind and loose, however, is also recorded two chapters later (Matthew 18:18). This time the "you" Jesus uses is plural. Binding and loosing devils, particularly higher levels of spiritual dominion, is not something you should tackle on your own.

Al Ells, a Christian psychologist and author, recounted to me an unusual story about the danger of what I call indiscriminate binding and loosing.

On his way to a meeting in downtown Phoenix, Al heard a radio news report of a recent court decision that struck him as decidedly humanistic. Indignant and an-gry, Al began to rebuke the principality behind the or-ganization responsible for bringing the issue before the court.

In a flash, Al had a vision of a huge, dark spirit reacting to the arrow of his prayer as it pierced its side. But it was a mini-arrow, and the giant spirit in the vision reacted violently, striking Al on the face. Al began immediately to experience intense pain in the right side of his face.

It was not until later in the day, when he received prayer from his counseling center staff, that he was released from the pain. Al learned an important lesson about spiritual warfare: He had challenged a significant dark power out of the boundary of his authority. Al was binding and loosing out of his anger, not out of the clear will of God.

Jesus implies this principle in His command to bind and loose. A more literal translation of the Greek text of Matthew 16:19 and 18:18 is: "Whatever you bind on earth will already have been bound in heaven, and whatever you loose on earth will already have been loosed in heaven."*

In other words, binding and loosing must always be in the will of God for a particular situation. A. T. Robertson, a widely recognized New Testament scholar, comments on Matthew 16:19 in *Word Pictures in the New Testament*, "All of this [that is, the unique grammatical construction in the Greek text] assumes, of course, that Peter's use of the keys will be in accord with the teaching and mind of Christ" (Vol. 1, p. 134).

Once after I preached on this subject, a woman in our church sent me this remarkable testimony, which I relay here with her permission:

> Several months ago I went over to [a Christian friend's] to pray through her house. I thought I was doing the "right thing" as there had been many problems in their home and marriage. However, I never stopped to ask the Lord if I *should* go. We prayed, did warfare (pulling down strongholds) . . . and went home. I was *physically* spent, so tired that I had to lie down for a nap. I didn't even want to talk to anyone.
>
> That night something happened. We awoke at 5:30 A.M. to find our house flooded with water! When we asked the Lord what happened, he said, "You stirred up a hornet's nest, and this is the result of it." He revealed how I did not

* *Will be bound* and *will be loosed* are translations of the future perfect indicative.

even ask him if I should have "cleaned" my friend's house.
Her husband was not in agreement and it was not God's
will for me to do warfare there.

There were things God wanted accomplished in that
family's order that I had interfered with. Well, the Lord
took care of the damage [of their water-soaked house], and
we learned an important lesson—to be obedient to the
Lord, our Commander and Chief.

Jesus commissions us to bind and loose, but we dare not
do it indiscriminately, whenever we have the urge. Spiritual warfare is serious business. Concerned about His disciples' carnal elation over their spiritual power, Jesus
cautioned them, "Do not rejoice that the spirits submit to
you, but rejoice that your names are written in heaven"
(Luke 10:20). We cannot expect to beat on the devil whenever we have the whim. But when we are called to act—
such as joining in prayer in a deliverance session for
another—we can do so with the knowledge that our words
carry authority.

Binding, Loosing and the Authority of the Church

We need to pray and intercede. We need to resist Satan,
and he will flee from us. But attacking him directly is
another matter. We must know our spiritual jurisdiction
and, if we are dealing with a particularly powerful principality, then we need the support and agreement of other
praying saints, which leads me to my next point: Binding
and loosing is directly related to the order and authority of
the Church.

The hierarchy of darkness understands authority and

chain of command far better than God's people. This is why rebellion or an attitude of independence in us is so dangerous. If our hearts are not dependent on God, then we are vying for His authority in our lives. Thus, we are to rely on God's authority—not our own—in order to rebuke the works of Satan.

Jude's little epistle is a stinging rebuke of those who "reject authority and slander celestial beings" (verse 8). To illustrate, Jude adds, "Even the archangel Michael . . . did not dare to bring a slanderous accusation against [the devil], but said, 'The Lord rebuke you!' " (verse 9). We cannot operate from God's authority and our own at the same time. A house divided against itself cannot stand. Anarchy will never overcome a carefully structured hierarchy.

It is not by accident, then, that the binding and loosing commission of Matthew 18:18 is preceded by instructions on authority and discipline in the Church (verses 15–17), and is followed by the promise,

> "If two of you on *earth* agree about anything you [plural] ask for, it will be done for you [plural] by my Father in *heaven* [note the references to "earth" and "heaven," parallel with verse 18]. For where *two or three* come together in my name, there am I with them."   Matthew 18:19–20

The community of other believers provides a protective covering for us. The fellowship of the saints is also a place of accountability. If there is sin in the church, we have the responsibility to confront with love and restore with gentleness: "If your brother sins against you, go and show him his fault, just between the two of you" (Matthew

18:15; see also Galatians 6:1). Sin is a doorway for the devil, and mutual accountability is a shelter in the spiritual storm.

An open and trusting relationship with another believer is like a mirror. Others around me allow me to see myself more clearly, if I am willing to look and listen. Just as "friends do not let friends drive drunk," so Christian friends do not let Christian friends come under the influence and dominion of darkness. A friend a day keeps the devil away. In other words, effective binding and loosing depends on the quality of our relationships with one another in the Body of Christ. One soldier cannot win a war. It takes an army.

Binding and Loosing and a Spirit of Forgiveness

We have looked at binding and loosing from the standpoint of spiritual warfare—binding the devil's power—but I should also mention that binding and loosing occur in relationships with fellow Christians. In that case, we wrongly bind a brother or sister by a spirit of unforgiveness toward them.

Open relationships work two ways: I must be open to correction and receiving forgiveness, and I must correct and forgive. To bind is to withhold forgiveness and redemption; to loose is to give it freely. In John's Gospel, Jesus gave the binding-loosing commission this relational twist: "If you forgive anyone his sins, they are forgiven; if you do not forgive them, they are not forgiven" (John 20:23).

The Greek word here translated "forgive" means "to release" and is a synonym of *luo* ("to loose"), and many

Greek authorities believe that John 20:23 is parallel with Matthew 16:19 and 18:18. Forgiveness looses the one who offends you from the guilt and penalty of your anger. Forgiveness is freedom. Unforgiveness binds both the unforgiving one and the unforgiven one. Unforgiveness is torment (Matthew 18:34).

Notice that Jesus told the parable of the unforgiving man (Matthew 18:22–35) in response to Peter's question, "How many times shall I forgive my brother when he sins against me?" (Matthew 18:21). And Peter asked the question so Jesus would clarify what He had just said about church discipline, binding and loosing, and the power of spiritual unity in prayer. Binding and loosing—of both fellow Christians and powers of darkness—have no power without the spirit of forgiveness.

In summary, how do we bind and loose? What are the keys of the Kingdom that lock and unlock? They are the finished work of Christ, seeking God's will, submission to the authority of the Church, and a spirit of forgiveness. If you feel these "conditions" are met, then you can speak rebuke to the devil and bind his evil power as the Lord leads you.

We will learn more about binding and loosing by the prayers we pray and by the praise we offer to God, two crucial topics to which I have devoted the final chapters of this book. But first let's look at demonization and ways to accomplish deliverances.

13

Demonization and Deliverance

"And these signs will accompany those who believe:
In my name they will drive out demons."

Mark 16:17

I was teaching a large group of people in a week-long discipleship school. My subjects were the gifts of the Spirit and the power of God. To supplement the lectures, I scheduled a spiritual gifts clinic one evening to demonstrate the reality and practice of the gifts.

The special presence of God was quite evident. A number of people asked for prayer, among them a young woman who had serious emotional problems. As I began to pray for her, she fell suddenly to the floor in what appeared to be a seizure.

It seemed to me that her problem was demonic, so I commanded the spirit to release her. Her body relaxed, and she began to cry. The next day she testified of the dramatic change that had happened in her life. Her countenance was noticeably transformed, and many of the people in the school who knew her well confirmed that she was acting like a different person.

Even though exorcism was a common feature of Jesus' ministry, the notion of demon possession is foreign to many Christians. But as Dickason writes in *Demon Posses-sion and the Christian*, "The New Testament and current events demonstrate the truth of demon invasion and con-trol of humans" (p.33).

Matthew and Dennis Linn have taught on healing in many countries and universities, including a course for doctors accredited by the American Medical Association. In the introduction to their book *Deliverance Prayer* Mat-thew Linn confesses his previous struggle to believe in the reality of demons today:

> Ten years ago I could not have edited this book. I knew that Christ called us to preach, heal and cast out demons in his name (Mk. 6:12–13; 16:15–18). I was willing to do the first two but didn't believe at all in demons. My graduate studies in anthropology, psychology and theology con-vinced me that demons were only to be found as gargoyles on medieval cathedrals or fantasies created by too much demon rum. . . .
>
> A growing number of doctors, psychiatrists and social workers now know that it is sometimes as necessary to treat demonic bondage with deliverance prayer as it is to treat bacteria with penicillin, a manic depressive neurosis with therapy and drugs, or an alcoholic with AA and en-vironmental change.
>
> Through the Association of Christian Therapists I have come to know over twelve hundred professionals who combine healing power, of which deliverance is a small but important part, with their professional practice (pp. 5, 7).

Jesus and Demons

If we believe that Jesus was God in the flesh, then we are bound to accept His world view, including His sensi-tivity to demon domination of human lives. Otherwise, we are left with a Jesus who was unwittingly influenced by primitive superstitions, an ignorant Jesus who is less than God. But to believe in Jesus is to believe in what He said and what He did, and He devoted a significant portion of His ministry to healing demon-possessed people.* Perhaps Matthew summarizes it best:

> Jesus went throughout Galilee, teaching in their synagogues, preaching the good news of the kingdom, and healing every disease and sickness among the people. News about him spread all over Syria, and people brought to him all who were ill with various diseases, those suffering severe pain, *the demon-possessed*, the epileptics and the paralytics, and he healed them.   Matthew 4:23–24

Jesus believed that demons play a significant role in human behavior, and that they must be driven out.

Demonization

Demons are elusive, but demons are real. They even have the ability to enter the life of a human being. Intertwining themselves with the personality of their victim, demons can control to one degree or another various aspects of the person's life. Dickason defines demonization as "demon-caused passivity or control due to a demon's residing within a person, which manifests its effects in various physical and mental disorders and in varying degrees" (p. 40).

---

* Other references to deliverance in Jesus' ministry: Matthew 8:28–34; 9:32–34; 12:22–29, 43–45; Mark 1:21–34, 39; 3:20–29; 5:1–20; 7:24–30; 9:14–29; Luke 4:31–36, 40–41; 8:26–38; 9:37–45; 10:17–20; 11:14–26; 13:10–17.

Using the story of the Gerasene demonic in Mark 5, Kurt Koch, the theologian who has co-written *Occult Bondage and Deliverance* with German psychiatrist Alfred Lechler, has identified eight distinct symptoms of demon possession:

1. The man was actually indwelt by another being (verse 2).

2. He had unusual power of physical strength (verse 3).

3. The possessed man had fits of rage (verse 4).

4. The fourth symptom is split personality. The demoniac ran to Jesus for help, yet cried out in fear (verses 6–7).

5. The man was resistant to the Christian faith and to spiritual ministry (verse 7). Koch notes here that "one meets this resistance to spiritual help quite often in counseling [demonized] people" (p. 58).

6. The sixth symptom is clairvoyant power. The possessed man knew immediately who Jesus really was (verse 7).

7. The man demonstrated a variation or alteration of voice. A "legion" of demons spoke out of him (verse 9).

8. The eighth characteristic is occult transference (verse 13).

Demons and Christians

Michael Scanlan, president of the University of Steubenville (Ohio), and co-author Randall J. Cirner have identified in *Deliverance from Evil Spirits* three ways that demons affect human persons: temptation, opposition and bondage (see pp. 27–35). We have seen how the dominion of darkness tempts and opposes the saints. As we noted, the apostle Peter warns us, "Be self-controlled and alert. Your enemy the devil [that is, the enemy of Christian believers] prowls around like a roaring lion looking for someone to devour. Resist him" (1 Peter 5:8–9).

A controversial question, however, has to do with the other way evil spirits affect people: bondage. Can a Christian be demon-possessed? The debate among Christians over this question will probably never be resolved, because the Bible does not address the question directly.

Yet I believe it is possible for a Christian to be demonized.* I think the woman mentioned at the beginning of this chapter and others I have ministered to have been bound by demonic power.

In her classic 1912 work on demons, *War on the Saints*, Jessie Penn-Lewis purports that

> Christians are as open to possession by evil spirits as other men, and become possessed because they have, in most cases, *unwittingly fulfilled the conditions upon which evil spirits work*. . . . The primary cause of deception and possession in surrendered believers may be condensed into one word, PASSIVITY: that is, a cessation of the active exercise of the will in control over spirit, soul and body . . . (p. 69).

Penn-Lewis goes on to distinguish between passivity, or the surrender of the will, and quietness, "or the 'meek and

---

* I have avoided using the term *possession*, because in the case of a Christian, he or she is "possessed" or owned by Christ alone. There is a point, however, at which a Christian's will may be ensnared by demon power. Thus, *demonization* is a term commonly used to describe demon influence beyond harassment.

quiet spirit,' which, in the sight of God, is of great price" (p. 71).

As I wrote in chapter 11, I learned about the reality and power of demons the hard way. Our whole church was a target, and I was the bull's eye. I have never experienced such powerful oppression and spiritual torment. There were times when some of us could "feel" a presence enter our church offices. An invisible cloud of dark resistance frequently visited our staff and elder prayer meetings.

Personally, I battled obsessive thoughts, especially about the validity of God's call on my life, and at times I was convinced God had abandoned me. But God gave me great grace, and with the temptations a way of escape so that—with the help of family and friends—I was able to endure them (1 Corinthians 10:13). Was I demonized? I don't believe so, although the dominion of darkness had enormous influence over my thoughts and feelings.

Perhaps no one has done a more thorough investigation than C. Fred Dickason. After study of Scripture, clinical considerations and an analysis of case studies, Dickason concludes,

> We must allow the distinct probability that biblically guided investigation and counsel has shown in experience that Christians have been demonized. The evidence is heavily weighted toward that conclusion (p. 186).

Deliverance

If demons inhabit people, then deliverance is a necessary aspect of Christian ministry. "And these signs will accompany those who believe: In my name they will drive out demons" (Mark 16:17).

Scanlan and Cirner suggest several types of deliverance (pp. 63 ff.).

Personal or self-deliverance is often possible through significant growth in personal holiness, or a person might minister to himself by commanding the evil spirits to leave in the name of Jesus.

Fraternal deliverance is when God works through Christian brothers and sisters to minister release from spiritual oppression.

The third type is *pastoral deliverance.* "When a person has pastoral responsibility for other people, the Lord gives that person the gifts and the authority to deal with deeper and more complex workings of evil spirits."

Fourth is *special ministry.* "God has given to some people special gifts of discernment, revelation and authority to overcome Satan and evil spirits at their most profound level of activity."

How do you cast out a demon?

First, ask yourself if it is a condition of demonization you can handle. If not, make a referral to someone who is competent in spiritual ministry, or you may wish to ask one or two others to assist you. If you are not sure, ask God if He is leading you to become involved.

Second, prepare yourself. Pray, asking for the anointing of power and the discerning of spirits. Jesus taught His disciples that some evil spirits do not respond to just anyone, anytime. Some people are delivered only after fervent prayer and fasting (Mark 9:29).

Third, ask the demonized person to prepare for ministry with prayer and fasting. This is not possible, of course, if the individual is heavily oppressed.

Fourth, minister deliverance privately whenever possible. If I am caught off-guard in a public meeting by an unexpected demonic manifestation, I always try to have the demonized person removed to another room. Demons seem to like attention. Furthermore, observing a deliverance can be very frightening to people who are not familiar with that kind of ministry.

Fifth, in the name of Jesus command the spirit, by name if necessary, to leave. Remember, the power of God has to do with Christ in you and the Spirit working through you, not the volume of your voice.

The Limitations of Deliverance

Deliverance is not a cure-all. Not every human problem has a demonic origin. James wrote, "When tempted, no one should say, 'God is tempting me.' For God cannot be tempted by evil, nor does he tempt anyone; but each one is tempted . . . [not by the devil, but] by his own evil desire" (James 1:13–14). Jesus addressed this when He declared, "For out of the heart come evil thoughts, murder, adultery, sexual immorality, theft, false testimony, slander" (Matthew 15:19).

Matthew Linn writes, "Those who see a need only for deliverance err just as greatly as those who see a need only for medicine, only for psychiatric treatment, or only for environmental change when several or all of these factors may contribute to a person's suffering" (p. 7). Demons are real. Demons influence human behavior. But never use demons as an excuse for personal sin or spiritual irresponsibility. Most human behavior is not demonic.

Deliverance does not always last. Even when a release from an evil spirit occurs, it does not guarantee permanent freedom. Deliverance must be accompanied by a commitment to obey God's Word and grow in Christ. Sometimes, if not always, personal accountability to other mature Christians is necessary during the transition period. Satan's government must be exchanged for God's, not just cast out. Jesus taught,

> "When an evil spirit comes out of a man, it goes through arid places seeking rest and does not find it. Then it says, 'I will return to the house I left.' When it arrives, it finds the house unoccupied, swept clean and put in order. Then it goes and takes with it seven other spirits more wicked than itself, and they go in and live there. And the final condition of that man is worse than the first."   Matthew 12:43–45

Deliverance does not always work. I have prayed for people to be delivered from what appeared to be unmistakably demonic symptoms, and their problems have not gone away. When praying with someone, we need to know not only when to begin, but when to stop. There may be other factors that require us to withdraw our forces in order to consider the problem from other angles. Sometimes it is a demon, sometimes it is not. Sometimes we lack faith, other times we don't.

The elusive, deceptive nature of demons can make deliverance ministry extremely complex.* Spiritual warfare is serious business, but keep asking God for discernment and power. If there is work to be done He will show you how to do it.

---

* Demonization and deliverance are not the primary subject of this book, and I have attempted to discuss a sensitive and difficult subject in a relatively short space. For further reading, I recommend the books cited in this chapter.

14
All Kinds of Prayer

And pray in the Spirit on all occasions with all kinds
of prayers and requests. With this in mind, be alert
and always keep on praying for all the saints.

Ephesians 6:18

We are living in what is perhaps the greatest prayer revival in history. In a recent issue of *Ministries Today* magazine (September/October 1989, p. 28), C. Peter Wagner declared that "the greatest prayer movement in living memory has already begun." Thousands of Christians and church leaders are gathering all over North America and around the world for special corporate prayer meetings.

The largest church in the history of Christianity, the Full Gospel Central Church in Seoul, South Korea, with more than half-a-million members, boasts 22 percent participation in corporate prayer. And in South America, which is also experiencing unprecedented revival, prayer is center stage. Traveling to Colombia in the summer of 1989, I spoke in Bogota's largest church, which has an estimated membership of more than twenty thousand.

I asked their pastor, Enrique Gomez, to tell me the secret of his success. "The power of Christ and prayer," he answered with conviction. About three thousand Christians gather there every Saturday morning for several hours of intense prayer.

According to Wagner there are bright beginnings here in North America, too. In 1988 in Minneapolis, for example, approximately ten thousand believers of every denominational persuasion, Catholics and Protestants alike, gathered for prayer and intercession for their state and nation. And in June of 1989, Larry Lea's Prayer Breakthrough in Anaheim, California, drew thousands to pray against the demonic powers that have been oppressing the Los Angeles area.

In my own city, Phoenix, an estimated seven thousand people attended early morning prayer meetings each day in conjunction with a citywide "Take It By Force" convention in August 1989. Two months later 26 churches in west Phoenix canceled their Sunday evening services to gather for corporate prayer at a high school football field. Currently, a number of pastors and Christian leaders here are developing a prayer strategy for our entire state.

The Weapon of Prayer

Pray! And then pray some more! Spiritual warfare is real and prayer has a militant purpose: to overcome the dominion of darkness in order to bring about change in people and society. The Kingdom of God is at hand, the abyss of darkness has been opened and the saints of God have a great weapon in prayer. We wrestle not with flesh-and-blood human problems. "With this in mind, be alert and always keep on praying for all the saints."

Ironically, even with growing world wide participation, prayer is something that the majority of Christians neglect with a passion. At least four times a year, our church devotes a full Sunday evening service to corporate prayer.

Regrettably, they are our most poorly attended public meetings. I am convinced that spiritual blindness is the basic cause of prayerlessness.

The more clearly you see the spiritual realm, the more you will pray; and conversely, the more you pray, the more you will see clearly the spiritual realm. A growing awareness of spiritual warfare will always bring with it an increasing commitment to pray. The two go hand in hand. Prayer puts us in touch with the spiritual dimension and releases the power of God. The deeply spiritual Andrew Murray wrote in *The Ministry of Intercession,*

> As one looks back on the history of the early church, how clear these two great truths stand out: 1) where there is much prayer, there will be much of the Spirit; and 2) where there is much of the Spirit, there will be ever-increasing prayer (p. 28).

Paul wraps up his discussion of spiritual warfare and weaponry in Ephesians 6 by making perhaps the most comprehensive and powerful declaration about prayer in all of Scripture. Here is my paraphrase of Ephesians 6:17–18:

> And all of you together take up the helmet of salvation, and the sword of the Spirit, the one that is the word [*rhema*] of God.* How do you do this? Through all prayer and petition, *praying constantly in every season, opportunity or crisis* in the Spirit, for the purpose of watching constantly** with all perseverance and prayer concerning all the saints.

* Or, "the sword of the Spirit, which is what God has spoken" (EMPHA-SIZED).
** The Greek term here means "sleeplessness."

The four lessons here, though simple, are critical. *First,* prayer is incredibly important. Notice that verse 18 on prayer explains *how* to take up the helmet and sword for battle. Without prayer there is no armor. Without prayer we are spiritually naked. Prayer is a matter of spiritual life and death.

Second, prayer in the Spirit is incredibly important. Prayer is a spiritual exercise, and the ultimate power of prayer is not how well you pray, or even how long you pray, but rather the participation of the Spirit. Jude echoes Paul's words: "Build yourselves up in your most holy faith and pray *in the Holy Spirit*" (Jude 20). The spirit power of the dominion of darkness must be confronted by the Spirit power of prayer. "The weapons we fight with are not the weapons of the world. On the contrary, they have divine power to demolish strongholds" (2 Corinthians 10:4).

Third, prayer is incredibly important in every situation. We are to pray constantly, without ceasing, "on all occasions." Can you imagine Jesus facing anything in life without first seeking the will of His Father? Everything in life, without exception, is an occasion for prayer, even if we are not dealing directly with a demon.

Fourth, all kinds of prayer are important. People often ask me, "*How* should I pray?" This question implies that prayer is a kind of spiritual formula: Get all the words right and God is bound to answer. It is as if Christians are playing a game of heavenly battleship, calling out grid numbers to God in hopes that He will say, "Hit."

How should I pray? I have a simple answer: Just pray! Then pray some more. Pray however you need to pray, as long as you need to pray, until you break through to God. "Pray in the Spirit on all occasions with all kinds of prayers and requests."

Elements of Prayer

The struggle, generally, is not so much knowing how to pray, but taking time to do it. Busyness has nothing to do with how many responsibilities you have; it is your state of mind. Jesus compassionately rebuked Mary's sister, "Martha, Martha . . . you are worried and upset about many things, but only one thing is needed. Mary has chosen what is better, and it will not be taken away from her" (Luke 10:41–42). Mary chose to sit in the presence of Jesus.

The practice of prayer is really very simple. "All kinds of prayers" have four common elements. *First*, prayer is talking with God. I am indebted to my wife, Marilyn, for this definition. Preparing a sermon series on prayer, I asked her to complete the sentence "Prayer is . . . ." Her immediate, simple and perfect answer: Prayer is talking with God. You can talk to God as you would a close friend. Without being afraid, you can tell Him exactly what you are thinking and feeling—or that you are confused and don't know what to think or feel.

Second, prayer is listening to God. Prayer is not frenzied begging. Listening prayer is quieting your soul, letting God converse with you out of the Scriptures. Listening prayer is opening your heart to God, allowing Him to speak into the ear of your spirit. When you hear God's voice, your thoughts will change, and when your thoughts change, your feelings and behavior will change.

Third, prayer is asking. "You do not have, because you do not ask God" (James 4:2). When your prayer requests are specific, it says two things about what you really believe. One, it demonstrates that you really believe there is a God. Two, it demonstrates that you believe God cares enough about you personally to answer your prayer.

Does this seem too simplistic? Too obvious? Turning the statement around uncovers the real issue. *Not* being specific in your prayers is a sign of unbelief. Generic prayers may give you a warm feeling, but they also give you and God an out. When you pray specific prayers it puts both you and God on the spot. The risk is that God might say no. But then He might say yes!

When our children were small, they never hesitated to ask us for specific things, regardless of how outrageous their requests may have been. And rarely did they take no for an answer. As kids get older, they get wiser—and more evasive. Kids learn how to ask for things more shrewdly because they are afraid they will get the wrong answer. But you cannot help your kids if you are not sure what they are asking.

God, of course, perceives all of our subtle intentions. He even knows our needs before we ask, but He still expects us to pray, and to pray specifically. It never hurts to ask. It may hurt when the answer is no, but being specific in prayer means that we must be open to the will of the Father, regardless of the answer. If you pray vague prayers, you may never know what God is saying. The writer of Hebrews declared, "Without faith it is impossible to please God, because anyone who comes to him must believe that he exists and that he rewards those who earnestly seek him" (Hebrews 11:6).

Fourth, prayer is believing. There is, of course, a difference between "just praying" (something I call "bedtime prayers") and passionate prayer. "The prayer *offered in faith,*" James writes, "will make the sick person well" (5:16). The King James translation refers to this as "effectual fervent" prayer. So important is our faith that even Jesus Himself, when faced with the lack of it in those around

Him, "could not do any miracles [in a certain place], except lay his hands on a few sick people and heal them. And he was amazed at their lack of faith" (Mark 6:5–6).

Intercession

Intercession is one of the many "kinds of prayer." Although the Greek terms for intercession (*enteuxis* and *entugchano*) are used sparingly in the New Testament and not at all in Ephesians 6, it is an important aspect of prayer. *Precede* means "go before"; *recede* means "go back"; *intercede* means "go between." Ezekiel voiced Jehovah's pain: "I looked for a man among them who would build up the wall and stand before me in the gap on behalf of the land so I would not have to destroy it, but I found none" (22:30).

Intercessory prayer is standing in the gap, becoming an intermediary in the spiritual realm. There is only one Mediator between God and man: Jesus Christ. But we become mediators of God's Kingdom when we intercede for our families, our friends and our nation, and work to break the powers of darkness over them. Intercession is redemptive praying, carrying us beyond our own selfish needs and bearing the burdens of others. In intercessory prayer, we merge with the very heart of God.

Intercession is sacrificial, fervent prayer, of which Jesus is our example: "He is able to save completely those who come to God through him, because he always lives to intercede for them" (Hebrews 7:25). Intercession is spiritual tenacity. The intensity of our intercession, however, is not measured by how much energy we expend, or how tired we are when the praying is over. The power of intercession is gauged by how persistently we pray and how sincerely we believe. As a conclusion to the parable of the persistent friend, Jesus declared,

> "Ask and keep on asking, and it shall be given you; seek and keep on seeking, and you shall find; knock and keep on knocking, and the door shall be opened to you. For every one who asks and keeps on asking receives, and he who seeks and keeps on seeking finds, and to him who knocks and keeps on knocking the door shall be opened."   Luke 11:9–10, TAB*

Furthermore, intercessory prayer is Kingdom activity. In prayer, believers draw on the powers of the age to come. The Kingdom power of prayer is unveiled in one of the most terrifying passages in the Bible, Revelation 8. John had had an earlier vision of martyred souls crying out to God, "How long, Sovereign Lord, holy and true, until you judge the inhabitants of the earth and avenge our blood?" (6:10). Revelation 8, a chilling panorama of global judgment, is the direct outcome of this prayer:

> Another angel, who had a golden censer, came and stood at the altar. He was given much incense [the aroma of Christ's finished work] to offer, with the prayers of all the saints, on the golden altar before the throne. The smoke of the incense, together with the prayers of the saints, went up before God from the angel's hand. Then the angel took the censer, filled it with fire from the altar, *and hurled it on the earth;* and there came peals of thunder, rumblings, flashes of lightning and an earthquake.   verses 3–5

---

* *The Amplified Bible* reflects the linear action of the Greek verbs used in these verses.

The implication here is that what happens on the earth is the direct aftermath of the prayers of the saints reaching the throne of God.

Masterful writer Eugene Peterson maintains in *Earth and Altar* that:

> Prayer is political action. Prayer is social energy. Prayer is public good. Far more of our nation's life is shaped by prayer than is formed by legislation. That we have not collapsed into anarchy is due more to prayer than to the police. . . . The single most important action contributing to whatever health and strength there is in our land is prayer. . . .
>
> We don't need a new movement to save America. The old movement is holding its own and making its way very well. . . . We don't need a new campaign, a new consciousness-raising, a new program, new legislation, new politics or a new reformation. The people who meet in worship and offer themselves in acts of prayer are doing what needs to be done (pp. 15, 21).

Prayer Changes Things

Prayer changes things. This is the not-so-obvious assumption of Paul's great challenge to pray on the battlefield of the spirit. If we wrestle with principalities and powers of darkness, then prayer is designed to accomplish something.

R. A. Torrey, influential in the founding of Biola University (California), wrote these words in *The Power of Prayer:*

> A very considerable proportion of the membership of our evangelical churches today do not believe even theoretically in prayer, that is, they do not believe in prayer as bringing anything to pass that would not have come to

pass even if they had not prayed. They believe in prayer as having a beneficial "reflex influence," that is, as benefitting the person who prays . . . but as for prayer bringing anything to pass that would not have come to pass if we had not prayed, they do not believe in it (p. 15).

There are numerous Scriptures that teach clearly that prayer changes *things*. James calls Elijah "a man just like us." He prayed earnestly that it would not rain, and it did not—for three-and-a-half years. Then he prayed again, and it rained. The lesson: "The prayer of a righteous man is powerful and effective." (See James 5:16–18.)

Even scientific inquiry has demonstrated that prayer changes things. An article in the January 20, 1989, issue of the *Journal of the American Medical Association* entitled "Positive Therapeutic Effects of Intercessory Prayer in a Coronary Unit Population" described measurable effects of prayer. Heart patients in a particular unit were randomly divided into two groups of approximately 200 each. The first group received prayer by Christians; the "control group" did not. The article states, "The control patients required ventilatory assistance, antibiotics, and diuretics more frequently than patients [receiving prayer]." It was a double-blind study, meaning neither doctors nor patients knew who was being prayed for. Prayer changes things!

Prayer Changes You

When you pray, you are placing yourself under the Lordship of Christ. Your priorities change. You change. In fact, the obedient, disciplined life of prayer is a statement about your personal priorities. As I said earlier, a priority is not what you think is important; it is what you do with your time. Prayer changes you three ways: spiritually, mentally/emotionally and physically.

First, prayer changes you spiritually. This is self-evident. The more time you spend in prayer, the more you will have a spiritual outlook. Jude's how-to for "[building] yourselves up in your most holy faith" was to "pray in the Holy Spirit" (verse 20). And R. A. Torrey penned these words:

> Prayer will promote our personal piety, our individual holiness, our individual growth into the likeness of our Lord Jesus Christ as almost nothing else. . . . Each time we commune with God we catch something new of His glory and reflect it out upon the world. . . . Here is the secret of becoming much like God, remaining long with God (pp. 18, 21).

If life is a spiritual battle, then we need spiritual power. Prayer makes us strong in the character of God and in the authority of Christ. Prayerlessness, on the other hand, increases our spiritual vulnerability.

Second, prayer changes you mentally and emotionally. Personal change is grounded in spiritual change. When you change spiritually by deepening your reliance on God, you change mentally and emotionally. To repeat a key spiritual warfare Scripture, "The weapons we fight with . . . have divine power to demolish strongholds," which include imaginations, arguments, pretensions—every thought that "sets itself up against the knowledge of God" (see 2 Corinthians 10:3–5).

Prayer brings us under the government of God, and where God rules there is peace. Isaiah put it this way: "Of the increase of his government *and peace* there will be no end" (9:7). And in another place and on a more personal level, the same prophet said, "You will keep in perfect peace him whose mind is steadfast, because he trusts in you" (26:3).

In an earlier chapter, I described a time of personal trauma. Spiritual warfare, coupled with God's demand for change in me and my own emotional upheaval, drove me to prayer and fasting. On one occasion, under the supervision and spiritual care of a Christian friend and counselor, I fasted for three days for release and emotional healing. Fasting is perhaps the most fervent way of praying.

During my fast, my wife's cousin visited us. He is an M.D. and not a professing Christian. Naturally, he was curious why I was refraining from a particularly delicious meal Marilyn had prepared. I thought for a moment. How was I going to explain fasting and spiritual warfare? And then it hit me: I was fasting, I told him, because I was going through a difficult time, and fasting is a personal discipline that helps me get on top of my emotions.

Others have told me the same thing: "The only way I can control my emotions is by fasting." Concentrated prayer and fasting can have a dramatically calming effect on emotions, and emotional stability is a key to victory in spiritual warfare. In contrast, emotional instability—anger; self-pity, fear—may become an open door to spiritual oppression. Nothing—not counseling, teaching cassettes, Christian television—*nothing* can substitute for fervent personal prayer. Jesus said, "This kind [of demon] does not go out except by prayer and fasting" (Matthew 17:21).*

---

* *Fasting* is not included in all translations. Actually, the textual evidence supporting the longer reading is quite strong. Without getting into a discussion of a very complex subject, I accept the longer reading as genuine. My view is based on Henry Sturz' thesis in *The Byzantine Text Type in New Testament Textual Criticism.*

Third, prayer changes you physically. Listen to the wonderful, familiar prophecy of Isaiah 40:

> The Lord is the everlasting God. . . .
> He gives strength to the weary
>   and increases the power of the weak.
> Even youths grow tired and weary,
>   and young men stumble and fall;
> but those who hope in the Lord
>   will renew their strength.
> They will soar on wings like eagles;
>   they will run and not grow weary,
>   they will walk and not be faint.
>
>   verses 28–30

How does prayer for physical healing work? *First,* it releases the power of God. God works directly through prayer. It was the power of God in the ministry of Jesus that healed the sick. Several times, the sicknesses that Jesus healed were associated with spirits of infirmity (Luke 13:10–17, for example), which points out even more clearly the need for spiritual power through prayer.

Second, prayer brings healing and health because it is the prototype of positive thinking. Dr. Art Mollen wrote in his syndicated newspaper column in December 1988,

> People weather emergencies in different ways. A few, unprepared for adversity, react angrily, looking to blame others. Such people lack spiritual health. They accumulate resentment with life's setbacks and may suffer from ulcers, heart attacks and cancer. Others grow from tragedies. They have the spiritual shoring up to handle difficulties and may even be healthier. . . .
>
> "Prayer is essentially a form of meditation that induces relaxation, including a decrease in the response of our nervous system," Dr. Herbert Benson writes in *Beyond the*

Relaxation Response: Harnessing the Healing Power of Your Personal Beliefs.

Regular prayer, like regular exercise, works best, he notes. It can improve digestive problems and insomnia; it can lower blood pressure, reducing tension headaches, irritability and fatigue; it may even prevent heart attacks.*

Drs. Mollen and Benson and others have merely rediscovered what the Bible has promised for thousands of years: "The prayer offered in faith will make the sick person well" (James 5:15). Scripture clearly affirms the relationship between spiritual well-being and physical health: "Do not be wise in your own eyes; fear the Lord and shun evil. This will bring health to your body and nourishment to your bones" (Proverbs 3:7–8). God's words of wisdom "are life to those who find them and health to a man's whole body" (Proverbs 4:22).

Prayer is talking, listening, asking, believing. Prayer is powerful. Prayer changes things. Prayer changes you—spiritually, emotionally and physically. Prayer is our source of strength and guidance in spiritual warfare. Therefore, "pray in the Spirit on all occasions with all kinds of prayer and requests. With this in mind, be alert and always keep on praying for all the saints." Pray. Pray often. Pray now:

Heavenly Father, teach me to pray. I realize that my problem is not ignorance but disobedience. Knowing how to pray is easy. Doing it is a spiritual battle in itself. Forgive me for my prayerlessness. Open my eyes to the spiritual realm so I will realize how necessary prayer is every day of my life. Help me to pray. Renew and deepen my prayer life. In the name of Jesus, who taught us to pray, Amen.

---

* Benson is not to my knowledge a professing Christian and is referring only to the physiological benefits of prayer.

15

Confronting the Difficulties of Prayer

We do not know what we ought to pray, but the Spirit himself intercedes for us with groans that words cannot express.   Romans 8:26

As the title of Dick Eastman's bestselling book on prayer proclaims, it is "no easy road." It is hard enough to establish a habit of prayer. But when you do and nothing happens to reward you for your effort, devastating discouragement may creep in. You may even begin resenting God. When you have prayed every way you know how, then what? Is Satan resisting you? Is he winning? Are you missing something? Have you forgotten to put on a piece of the armor?

The Frustration of Not Knowing How to Pray

Prayer is not a bag of spiritual tricks. Prayer reduced to a formula is not prayer. After reading every book on the subject, after experimenting with every technique and exploring every prayer "secret," sometime, sooner or later, inevitably you will come to a sense of helplessness and frustration.

What then? Read just one more book? Memorize one more Scripture? Get just a little more faith? Like Job's counselors, our well-meaning Christian friends will keep trying to help us discover the "ultimate cause" of our problem.

What we have to realize is that some situations defy ultimate explanations. The apostle Paul wrote, "We know in part and we prophesy in part" (1 Corinthians 13:9). When we have done our very best, we are still weak warriors. In this present age, no matter how spiritually sensitive and wise we become, this is the reality: "We are looking in a mirror that gives only a dim (blurred) reflection [of reality as in a riddle or enigma]" (1 Corinthians 13:12, TAB). We pray in part, and sometimes we do not know how to pray at all.

A member of my church handed me this little story from the business publication *Bits and Pieces* (Vol. I, No. 6):

> An elderly gentleman passed his granddaughter's room one night and overheard her repeating the alphabet in an oddly reverent way. "What on earth are you up to?" he asked.
>
> "I'm saying my prayers," explained the little girl. "But I can't think of exactly the right words tonight, so I'm just saying all the letters. God will put them together for me, because he knows what I'm thinking."

This reminded me of Jesus' pronouncement, "I am the Alpha and the Omega,* the Beginning and the End" (Rev-

---

* Alpha and omega are the first and last letters of the Greek alphabet.

elation 21:6). Jesus is everything in the middle, too. He is God's encyclopedia of answers for human problems. When all that we can muster is a garbled prayer, God puts the sounds and letters together.

"In the same way, the Spirit helps us in our weakness. We do not know what we ought to pray, but the Spirit himself intercedes for us with groans that words cannot express" (Romans 8:26). The King James reads, "For we know not what we should pray for as we ought," suggesting two of the most frustrating aspects of prayer: not knowing what to pray and not knowing how. *The Amplified Bible* points this out as well: "For we do not know what prayer to offer *nor* how to offer it worthily as we ought."

This verse about the Spirit's intercession is in the middle of what is widely considered one of the most important chapters in the Bible—Romans 8. A few highlights from this chapter, then, are important for understanding verse 26.

First, life can be a real mess. Paul writes,

> The creation waits in eager expectation for the sons of God to be revealed. For the creation was subjected to frustration, not by its own choice, but by the will of the one who subjected it, in hope that the creation itself will be liberated from its bondage to decay and brought into the glorious freedom of the children of God.
>
> We know that the whole creation has been groaning as in the pains of childbirth right up to the present time. Not only so, but we ourselves, who have the firstfruits of the Spirit, groan inwardly as we wait eagerly for our adoption as sons, the redemption of our bodies.
>
> verses 19–23

Simply stated, life is not what it ought to be, nor is it what it will be. Life is difficult at best, and we are all groaning for a better world. The whole world groans.*

I was asked to do a funeral for a family I did not know. It was as sad a service as I have ever seen. A mother and her 24-year-old invalid child were in a serious car accident that killed the mother. At the close of the service, a family member rolled the daughter's wheelchair to the side of the coffin.

I wasn't sure she could understand what was happening—until she broke into the most pathetic weeping I have ever heard. I cried. Everyone cried. The woman in the coffin had spent all her waking hours lovingly caring for a human being who would now probably have to be institutionalized.

What do you say in a situation like that? What do you pray? It is no wonder that Paul declared, "I consider that our present sufferings are not worth comparing with the glory that will be revealed in us." Paul is idealistic in the proper sense, but he is also realistic. Life is so difficult at times, the warfare so intense, that "we know not what we should pray for as we ought." We don't know what to say. We don't know what to pray. We don't know how to pray.

The only hope for a groaning cosmos, according to Romans 8, is God's threefold provision: First, the certainty of the resurrection and ultimate renewal of the entire universe (verses 20–23); second, the promise that somehow

---

* We are more conscious of this at the end of the twentieth century than ever before in human history. The globe is staggering under the curse of sinful, wasteful, thoughtless, shortsighted humankind. Howard Snyder in his book *Foresight: Ten Major Trends that Will Dramatically Affect the Future of Christians and the Church* lists as one of those trends moving "from threatened nations to threatened planet."

everything will work together for good for those who love God (verse 28); and third, the constant intercession of the Holy Spirit (verse 27). When we don't know how to pray or what to pray or can't pray, the Spirit intercedes on our behalf with a groaning of empathy and power that overcomes the groanings of a dark world.*

What does this have to do with spiritual warfare? Paul's conclusion in Romans 8:34–39 is clear:

> Christ Jesus . . . is at the right of God *and is also interceding for us.* Who [then] shall separate us from the love of Christ? . . . I am convinced that neither death nor life, neither angels *nor demons,* neither the present nor the future, nor any powers [social, political *or spiritual*], neither height nor depth, nor anything else in all creation, will be able to separate us from the love of God that is in Christ Jesus our Lord.

When you feel the dominion of darkness is closing in on you, and it seems you are losing the battle, *fear not!* Jesus is praying for you. Two powerful passages in the Bible, one in the Old Testament and one in the New, illustrate

---

* Romans 8:26 is thought by many to be a reference to speaking in tongues, or glossolalia. I disagree. It is quite clear that the groanings of the Spirit are not expressible in words. They cannot be uttered. Speaking in tongues may sound like groaning, but it is groaning that can be expressed and heard. The groaning of the Spirit is silent to the human ears, just like the other "groanings" to which Paul refers in this passage (see verses 22–23). Furthermore, the Greek preposition *huper* used twice by itself in verses 26 [variant reading] and 27, and once in the compound verb *huperentuchano* (verse 26), means "over," or "in behalf of." Speaking in tongues is the Holy Spirit praying *in* us and *through* us, not *over* us. I believe that speaking in tongues is a valid gift in the Church today (see my first book *And Signs Shall Follow*) but what we believe about tongues must be based on passages other than Romans 8:26. Speaking in tongues is not unrelated, however, to the intercession of the Spirit, because it is a wonderful spiritual exercise when you do not know what to pray or how to pray.

the effectual intercessory work of Christ in the spiritual battle for your soul. The first is Zechariah 3, where "Joshua the high priest [is] standing before the angel of the Lord, and Satan [is] standing at his right side to accuse him" (verse 1).

In the historical setting, many Israelites were returning from Babylonian exile to rebuild the city of Jerusalem and the Temple of Jehovah, destroyed some seventy years earlier. Joshua, the current high priest of the new Israel,* represented the pinnacle of spirituality, the cream of the Jewish nation. But his religious best was not good enough, because "Joshua was dressed in filthy clothes as he stood before the angel" (verse 3). Satan really had the right to accuse him!

When I look at my life, even the best days of my walk with God, I know that it is impossible to avoid some kind of attitude or thought that would give Satan cause to accuse me. So when the answers to my prayers are delayed, my failures—sometimes the littlest ones—stare me in the face. It is precisely these failures that Satan targets with his vicious accusations and killer condemnation.

We try desperately to close every door, but Satan knows what's in our closets. Self-cleansing is spiritually self-defeating. Our only certain defense against the dominion of darkness is the angel of the Lord, Jesus Christ, interceding for us as He did for Joshua. "The Lord said to Satan, 'The Lord rebuke you, Satan! The Lord, who has chosen Jerusalem, rebuke you!' " (verse 2). Romans 8:33 echoes, "Who will bring any charge against those whom God has chosen?"

---

* This is not the Joshua who fought the battle of Jericho.

Next, the angel of the Lord deals with Joshua's sins:

> [He] said to those who were standing before him,
> "Take off his filthy clothes." Then he said to Joshua,
> "See, I have taken away your sin, and I will put rich
> garments on you." Then [he] said, "Put a clean tur-
> ban on his head." So they put a clean turban on his
> head and clothed him, while the angel of the Lord
> stood by.   verses 4–5

All of this prefigures the work of Christ in the New
Testament. He exchanges the filthy rags of our own works
(Isaiah 64:6) for the glistening, spotless robe of His righteousness (Revelation 19:7–8). "Therefore he is able to
save *completely* those who come to God through him, *because he always lives to intercede for them*" (Hebrews 7:25).

The story of Peter's triple denial is another equally dramatic illustration of the power of Christ's intercession for
us in the battle for our souls. Before His crucifixion, Jesus
pierced Peter's heart with a painful prophecy: "Simon,
Simon, Satan has asked to sift you as wheat. *But I have
prayed for you,* Simon, that your faith may not fail. And
when you have turned back, strengthen your brothers"
(Luke 22:31–32).

From my point of view there are times when my faith,
like Peter's, seems to fail. It looks as though Satan has won
and I have become the victim of his schemes. But this
story of Peter and Jesus' prayers for him offers comfort.
When my relationship with God, from my end of things,
goes into remission, Jesus is still praying that my faith will
not fail. The incense of Christ's sacrifice on Calvary is
mingled with my feeble prayers, so that by the time they
reach the throne of God, all my words and letters—like the

little girl's in the story—have been rearranged (see Revelation 8:1–4).

Jesus even commanded Peter to strengthen his brothers after the ordeal of his denial! How could Peter strengthen anyone? He was a failure. He willfully and maliciously denied Jesus three times. But Peter learned an unforgettable lesson in grace. His testimony to his brothers was that, while his *own* strength failed, the intercessory prayer of Jesus shielded his soul from satanic penetration.

I am a conqueror in spiritual warfare, ultimately, not because *my* faith endures, but because Jesus prays for my faith to endure. When you don't know what to pray, or how to pray, or don't even feel like praying, the Holy Spirit is interceding for you with inexpressible groanings. And so is Jesus. If God be for us, who in heaven, earth or hell can stand against us! "We are more than conquerors *through him*" (Romans 8:37). "Thanks be to God, who *always* leads us in triumphal procession in Christ" (2 Corinthians 2:14).

The Guilt of Unanswered Prayer

If I have done everything I know to do, and Jesus is praying for me, why are some prayers never answered? Just today, a woman in our church called for comfort and to ask if I would conduct her husband's funeral. A Christian, this man had been seriously injured in a 1980 car wreck in which he was intoxicated. His life since the accident was a roller coaster of seizures and more drinking. It was a seizure that killed him.

His wife has been praying for years. (He prayed, too—when he was not overwhelmed by guilt.) Prayer is supposed to change things. Did their prayers fail? Did Jesus' prayers fail? Did Satan win?

Prayer, faith, healing ministry, resisting the devil and his dominion of darkness—all are related concepts. And, all things being equal, when they don't "work," it raises perhaps the most difficult issues of the Christian life. At the root is the age-old question, Why does tragedy happen to good people? If we are "good," why do our prayers of faith remain unanswered? Why does evil seem to win? I don't have all the answers, but I have some ideas that have helped me.

A foundational principle of Christianity is that faith works. That is why we pray. Resist the devil and he will flee from you, for greater is Jesus in you than the devil in the world. I diagram it this way:

$$\text{Faith} \longrightarrow \text{Results}$$

Faith produces results. This is simple logic, evidenced by numerous verses. Hebrews 11:6 is particularly clear on this point: "Without faith it is impossible to please God, because anyone who comes to him must believe that he exists and that he rewards those who earnestly seek him."

But here is where the simple logic breaks down. We know this is true:

$$\text{Faith} \longrightarrow \text{Results}$$

We assume, then, that this is also true:

$$\text{No Faith} \longleftarrow \text{No Results}$$

No result, we think, is a sure sign that there is no faith, or at least not enough faith—or prayer or spiritual power.

The effect of this is discouragement or alarm or a sense of failure and defeat or even a waning trust in God.

A young couple in our church were expecting their third child. Every indicator pointed to a normal pregnancy but, unexpectedly, the mother-to-be began experiencing premature labor. She was rushed to the hospital and gave birth to a little boy with severe genetic deformities.

I was the first one they called. They were so distraught they wanted personal counsel and ministry before asking their family to visit and see the child. I will never forget the very first thing this young, suffering mother asked me: "Do you think something wrong in me allowed this to happen?"

"No," I responded with firm conviction, remembering the man born blind and Jesus' words that sin in his parents was not the reason (see John 9). "This is difficult enough without your having to bear false guilt." She was actually thinking that this horrible personal crisis was caused by some moral or spiritual lack on her part. No results, or in this case bad results, was interpreted by this couple as a lack of faith.

Hebrews 11 is probably the most lengthy and thorough treatment of overcoming faith in the Bible. After the well-known definition of faith in verse 1, the writer surveys the practice and power of faith in the lives of an assortment of Old Testament heroes. As we might expect, most of the examples in the chapter demonstrate that faith produces results: "*Through faith* [they] conquered kingdoms, administered justice, and gained what was promised" (verse 33).

But notice the change in the middle of verse 35: The list of "successful" saints ends with the first half of the verse: "Women received back their dead, raised to life again." Now almost imperceptibly the ballad changes to a minor key: "*Others* were tortured and refused to be released. . . . They were stoned; they were sawed in two; they were put to death by the sword. They went about in sheepskins and goatskins, destitute, persecuted and mistreated."

Did the dominion of darkness win? Was something wrong with their faith? No! In fact, these "were all commended for their faith, yet none of them received what had been promised" (verse 39). Faith, then, is not measured by tangible results alone. Sometimes it is measured by perseverance, even when there are no visible results! Earlier in Hebrews 11 we find these words about those we consider "successful" in their faith: "All these people were still living by faith when they died. They did not receive the things promised; they only saw them and welcomed them from a distance" (verse 13).

Matthew 13 is a unique explanation of this contradiction. In this chapter Jesus presents the parables of the Kingdom. Remember that spiritual warfare is a clash of the kingdoms. Surprisingly, these parables do not seem to be about the wonderful success of God's Kingdom, but of its impurities and apparent failures. Seeds that seem to be wasted (verses 3–23). Yeast in the dough (verse 33). A net that caught "all kinds of fish," good and bad (verses 47–50).

In other words, Jesus is teaching His disciples how to face *failure in the Kingdom* realistically. The parable of the wheat and the weeds (verses 24–30, 37–43) illustrates this most profoundly: "The kingdom of heaven is like a man who sowed good seed in his field. But while everyone was sleeping, his enemy came and sowed weeds among the wheat."

Jesus explains, "The one who sowed the good seed is the Son of Man. The field is the world, and the good seed stands for the sons of the kingdom. The weeds are *the sons of the evil one*, and the enemy who sows them *is the devil*." The servants ask the owner of the field, "Do you want us to go and pull them up?" "No," he answers, "because while you are pulling the weeds, you may root up the wheat with them. Let them both grow together until the harvest."

Let them both grow together? How could Jesus say this? It is an important lesson: We have to learn to live with the possibility of failure, even in spiritual warfare. Now this does not mean that we give up! Winning in life is walking with God even when it looks as if you are not winning— not just when the problems go away. Paul put it this way: "I know what it is to be in need, and I know what it is to have plenty. I have learned the secret of being content in any and every situation, whether well fed or hungry, whether living in plenty or in want" (Philippians 4:12).

Thus, aggressive spiritual warfare—casting out demons, pulling down strongholds—is not the only way to overcome the dominion of darkness. Satan is foiled when we insist on praising God, even when we are engulfed in suffering.

> Though the fig tree does not bud and there are no grapes on the vines, though the olive crop fails and the fields produce no food, though there are no sheep in the pen and no cattle in the stalls, yet I will rejoice in the Lord, I will be joyful in God my Savior.
> Habakkuk 3:17–18

Persistent faith in the face of adversity is a great victory. "Even in darkness light dawns for the upright. . . . His heart is secure, he will have no fear; *in the end* he will look in triumph on his foes" (Psalm 112:4, 8).

Job stood his ground, even though Satan had brought him to the brink of destruction. Ecclesiastes, much like Job, is a book of unanswered questions about the inconsistencies of life. The book begins, "Meaningless! Meaningless! . . . Utterly meaningless! Everything is meaningless" (Ecclesiastes 1:2). And yet the writer, Solomon, looking straight into the eye of life's injustice, commands, "Fear God and keep his commandments, for this is the whole duty of man" (12:13).

You can be victorious in warfare if you are willing to persevere when things look the darkest. Prayer strengthens you in the battle and brings the towers of the enemy toppling down—whether you can see it or not. As Jesus told His disciples, we "should *always pray and not give up*" (Luke 18:1).

We will win in the end.

16

The Kingdom Power of Praise

> May the praise of God be in their mouths and a double-edged sword in their hands, to inflict vengeance on the nations and punishment on the peoples, to bind their kings with fetters, their nobles with shackles of iron, to carry out the sentence written against them. Psalm 149:6–9

Worship is the ultimate issue of the universe. Whoever or whatever gets worshiped, directly or indirectly, becomes the higher authority of the one worshiping. And wherever there is acknowledgment of a higher authority, there is control and dominion—a kingdom.

Praise is Kingdom activity. Praise to Jesus is an aggressive affirmation before the audiences of heaven, earth and hell that He is Lord! It is both the confession of your mouth (speaking, singing) that Jesus is Lord *and* a lifestyle of obedience and service to Him.

Over against the true worship, Satan's ageless obsession has been to depose God and redirect the adoration of the universe to himself. In what is widely believed to be a reference to the downfall of Satan, Isaiah writes,

How you have fallen from heaven, O morning star
[*Lucifer* in the KJV], son of the dawn! . . . You who
once laid low the nations! You said in your heart, "I
will ascend to heaven; I will raise my throne above
the stars of God; I will sit enthroned on the mount of
assembly, on the utmost heights of the sacred mountain. . . . I will make myself like the Most High."

Isaiah 14:12–14

When Jesus came to reestablish God's Kingdom in the
earth, Satan shrewdly offered Him a shortcut to victory,
an easy way out of the cross. He proposed to give Jesus
authority over all the kingdoms of this world in exchange
for a few moments of worship. Satan knew that an instant
of praise from the Son of God would have had unimagin-
able consequences.

Whom *you* praise and what *you* worship have enormous
implications, because whomever or whatever you worship
will become the master of your soul. Listen to the frightful
conditions of the last days: "The whole world was astonished and followed the beast [the Antichrist]. *Men worshiped the dragon* because he had given authority to the
beast, *and they also worshiped the beast*" (Revelation 13:3–4).

The terrible result: the beast gained absolute control over
their lives. A second beast, a kind of unholy spirit, gives
life to the son of Satan:

He was given power to give breath to the image of the
first beast, so that it could speak and cause all who
refused to worship the image to be killed. He also
forced everyone, small and great, rich and poor, free
and slave, to receive a mark on his right hand or on
his forehead, so that no one could buy or sell unless
he had the mark.

Revelation 13:15–17

Worship is not just the songs you sing. It is the submission of your life to a higher power. Jesus says it very simply: "No one can serve two masters. Either he will hate the one and love the other, or he will be devoted to the one and despise the other. You cannot serve both God and Money" (Matthew 6:24).

The Greek term Jesus uses for *money* is *mamonas*, or "mammon." Kittel's *Theological Dictionary of the New Testament* indicates that this word seems to come from an Aramaic* root that means "that in which one trusts" (p. 55). And what you worship you will trust. The object of your worship will become the focus of your faith—like alcohol or your job or money. And what you worship will rule your life.

Praise and God's Presence

How important are praise and worship to God? In Psalm 87 we discover that the Lord loves the gates of Zion more than all the dwellings of Jacob (verse 2). All the dwellings *of Jacob?* We might expect the psalmist to write that God loves the gates of Zion more than all the dwellings of Egypt or Assyria. But instead, he compares God's feelings about Zion, or Jerusalem, with the other cities and villages of Jacob, that is, Israel.

What does this mean, that God favors Zion over the other dwellings of Israel? Isn't He omnipresent? Why would He prefer one place to another? The Bible teaches that God is particular about where He reveals His *special* presence, something the Jews called the shekinah. The shekinah could be found in only one place: above the Ark

* Aramaic, a kind of Hebrew dialect, was the common language spoken by Jesus and His disciples.

of the Covenant in the Holy of Holies in the Tabernacle
and later in the Temple. In conjunction with this, God's
special shekinah presence became associated with the cap-
ital city and spiritual stronghold of the nation of Israel.

Psalm 87 tells us specifically that God loves *the gates* of
Zion more than all the dwellings of Jacob. What about the
gates that attract God's attention? A prophecy about the
future glory of Zion, Isaiah 60 opens with the proclama-
tion, "Arise, shine [Zion], for your light has come, and the
glory of the Lord [His special presence] rises upon you"
(verse 1).

Later in the chapter Zion's gates are clearly identified:
"You will call your walls Salvation *and your gates Praise*"
(verse 18). Praise is the gateway into the presence of God.
In another place the psalmist declares, "Shout for joy to
the Lord, all the earth. Serve the Lord with gladness; come
before him with joyful songs. . . . *Enter his gates with
thanksgiving and his courts with praise*" (Psalm 100:1–2, 4).

Praise is also God's dwelling place: "But thou art holy,
O thou that inhabitest the praises of Israel" (Psalm 22:3,
KJV). Another translation reads, "Yet Thou art holy, O
Thou who art enthroned upon the praises of Israel" (NAS).

This points us toward the New Testament. In the Gospel of John we read that a Samaritan woman queried Jesus
about the proper place to worship. To put it another way,
she was asking the Messiah, "Where is God's special
dwelling place, because that's where I want to worship?"

Jesus surprised her by abandoning the age-old idea of
worship being restricted to a particular mountain or high
place. Instead, He predicted, "A time is coming and has
now come when the true worshipers will worship the Father in spirit and truth, for they are the kind of worshipers
the Father seeks" (John 4:23). Jesus taught that Zion is

spiritual, not geographical. The dwelling place of God is worship—in spirit and in truth. (See also 1 Peter 2:4–6.)

To take this a step further, the shekinah in the Old Testament can be associated with the coming of the Spirit in the New. The shekinah is the presence and power of the Holy Spirit, and where you have the presence of the Holy Spirit, you have God's power and Kingdom. Over a period of forty days after His resurrection, Jesus spoke with His disciples about the Kingdom of God (Acts 1:3). During this time and out of these discussions He promised, "You will receive power [Kingdom authorization] when the Holy Spirit comes on you" (Acts 1:8).

A few days later in fulfillment of Jesus' prediction, the Spirit fell on the disciples. A significant outcome was powerful, spontaneous worship: "We hear them declaring the wonders of God in our own tongues!" (Acts 2:11). The dwelling place of God's special presence in the New Testament is His worshiping Church. Pentecost is the special presence and power of God to empower Christians to do the work of the Kingdom. It is also the rich experience of spiritual worship.

It is no coincidence, then, that the present international outpouring of the Spirit* has been similarly accompanied by a renewal in worship. When the Spirit comes in power,

---

* Renowned researcher David B. Barrett reported in the *International Bulletin of Missionary Research*, July 1988, that the modern Pentecostal movement in its great diversity of expression has grown to 332 million members worldwide, including 66 percent membership in the third world, the majority of the world's megachurches and two-thirds of global evangelism plans. The renewal of the Spirit in our generation is not only the greatest expansion of Pentecostalism in history; it has been called the greatest global renewal of the Church in history. This information is derived from the magazine *A.D. 2000 Together*. Its source was Stanley M. Burgess and Gary B. McGee, eds., *Dictionary of Pentecostal and Charismatic Movements* (Grand Rapids: Zondervan, 1988).

people worship. And when the people worship, the Spirit comes in power.

The Weapon of Praise

Worship is humanity's highest calling. Human worship is the throne and dwelling place of the almighty God. On the other side, worship is a powerful weapon in spiritual warfare that dethrones the devil. "From the lips of children and infants you have ordained praise because of your enemies, *to silence the foe and the avenger*" (Psalm 8:2).

We have already seen that praise is the gateway to God's special presence. In the Bible, gates are also symbolic of authority and power. In an earlier chapter, I discussed how *the gates of Hades* in Matthew 16:18 refers to the counsels or schemes of demonic authority. Gates, then, represent a place of control. I refer again to Kittel's authoritative *Dictionary of New Testament Theology:*

> The most likely meaning is that the gates of Hades stand for the ungodly forces of the underworld which attack the rock but cannot prevail against it. Later the "gates of Hades" figure especially in references to Christ's descent into Hades, *over whose gates he has supreme power* (pp. 974– 975, italics added).

Indeed, with eyes of fire the resurrected Christ decrees, "I am the Living One; I was dead, and behold I am alive for ever and ever! And I hold the keys of death and Hades" (Revelation 1:18). It is in this context that Psalm 127:5 takes on special meaning: "Blessed is the man whose quiver is full of [children]. They will not be put to shame when they contend with their enemies *in the gate*." Gates are not only symbolic of authority; they represent the place where that authority is challenged.

Perhaps nothing teaches the power of praise more clearly than Psalm 149. The whole thrust of this psalm is the primacy and power of praise and worship, but it ends with one of the most extraordinary statements in the Bible:

> May the praise of God be in their mouths and a double-edged sword in their hands, to inflict vengeance on the nations and punishment on the peoples, to bind their kings with fetters, their nobles with shackles of iron, to carry out the sentence written against them. This is the glory of all his saints.
>
> verses 6–9

When used in conjunction with the double-edged sword of the Word (compare Hebrews 4:12), praise is a weapon. By worship and the Word we overcome the dominion of darkness, which holds the nations in its oppressive grip. By worshiping, we actually participate in God's judgment over the earth: "This is the glory of all his saints."

The Hebrew term translated "glory" is *hadar*, which means "ornament" or "splendor." According to R. Laird Harris in the *Theological Wordbook of the Old Testament* this word is associated, among other things, with the glory of nature and man as they reflect the glory and goodness of God. When we use praise as a weapon to bind Satan's power in the earth, we are fulfilling God's purpose for creating humans: to have dominion.

This same Hebrew word is used in Psalm 8: "What is man that you are mindful of him . . . ? You . . . crowned him with glory and honor [*hadar*]. *You made him ruler over the works of your hands; you put everything under his feet"* (verses 4–6). It is the great honor of the saints to represent God in the earth by exercising authority over the dominion of darkness.

Psalm 47 is another passage that demonstrates the relationship between praise and spiritual authority: "Clap your hands, all you nations; shout to God with cries of joy. . . . He subdued nations *under us*, peoples under our feet" (verses 1, 3). Praise and worship are the alternating links in the chain that binds Satan and the forces of hell. *Praise is Kingdom activity.*

If you are in a spiritual battle, read the incredible story of warfare and victory in 2 Chronicles 20. Notice especially the importance of praise and worship in verses 18–22. Then pray and affirm one or more of the following triumphant Kingdom psalms: 2, 46, 47, 100, 110.

Speak these psalms aloud as a confession to build your faith. Speak them aloud to the audience of heaven, earth and hell. Do it daily, or even several times a day, if your situation demands it.

> Sing praises to God, sing praises;
>   sing praises to our King, sing praises.
> For God is the King of all the earth;
>   sing to him a psalm of praise.
> God reigns over the nations;
>   God is seated on his holy throne.
>
> Psalm 47:6–8

Praise and the Coming Kingdom

Old Testament prophecy even suggests that the establishment of the messianic Kingdom will be uniquely characterized by praise and worship. When the Kingdom is fully established, the ultimate issue of the universe—worship, the thing the devil wants to secure—will be settled forever. Psalm 102 points forward to a messianic Kingdom headquartered in the heavenly Jerusalem: "You will arise and have compassion on Zion, for it is time to show favor to her; the appointed time has come" (verse 13).

At this time, "the nations will fear the name of the Lord, all the kings of the earth will revere your glory. . . . So the name of the Lord will be declared in Zion and his praise in Jerusalem when the people and the kingdoms assemble *to worship the Lord*" (verses 15, 21–22).

This prophecy has a twofold significance. First, it refers to the Gospel of the Kingdom that will be preached to all nations. No longer will Jehovah's influence be limited to little Israel, but the fame of His name will cover the earth as the waters cover the sea. This happens when we obey the Great Commission to disciple the nations.

Second, the prophecy of Psalm 102 points toward the ultimate and total triumph of Christ over the nations, when the reign and rule of God will be established in a new heaven and a new earth. All the groaning will be silenced, and the whole creation will be released into the liberty of Christ. All the earth will bow down in unrestrained worship to God and the Kingdom of God will be established forever.

No longer will there be two masters. Satan will be thrown into the lake of fire forever. Paul puts it this way: "Therefore God exalted [Jesus] to the highest place and gave him the name that is above every name, that at the name of Jesus every knee should bow, in heaven and on earth and under the earth" (Philippians 2:9–10).

Until the Grand Ending, however, the Kingdom is

among us and at hand. As Ron Ford has written in an article entitled, "The Powerful Advance of God's Kingdom in the Earth" (*First Fruits*, January/February 1986, p. 16), "We are living in *the presence of the future.* . . . The Kingdom of God *is* where the rule and reign of God is exercised and made visible." And the reign of God is made visible where people worship in word and deed.

Worship is the ultimate issue of the universe. Worship is perhaps the most powerful and liberating weapon in spiritual warfare. Worship affirms the Lordship of Jesus Christ over all creation and casts down the dominion of darkness.

Bibliography

Spiritual Warfare

Barnhouse, Donald Grey. *The Invisible War*. Grand Rapids: Zondervan, 1965.

Basham, Don. *Deliver Us from Evil*. Old Tappan, N.J.: Chosen Books, 1972.

Bubeck, Mark I. *The Adversary*. Chicago: Moody, 1975.

———. *Overcoming the Adversary*. Chicago: Moody, 1984.

Dickason, C. Fred. *Demon Possession and the Christian*. Westchester, Ill.: Crossway, 1987.

———. *Demon Experiences in Many Lands*. Chicago: Moody, 1960.

Groothuis, Doug. *Confronting the New Age*. Downers Grove, Ill.: InterVarsity, 1988.

———. *Unmasking the New Age*. Downers Grove, Ill.: InterVarsity, 1986.

Koch, Kurt. *Christian Counseling and Occultism*. Grand Rapids: Kregel, 1972.

Koch, Kurt and Alfred Lechler. *Occult Bondage and Deliverance*. Grand Rapids: Kregel, 1971.

Laine, James A. *A Biblical View of Demonology*. n.p., 1981.

———. *The Weapons of Our Warfare: Help for Troubled Minds*. New Wilmington, Penn.: Son-Rise, 1986.

Lindsell, Harold. *The World, the Flesh, and the Devil*. Minneapolis: World Wide Publications, 1973.

Linn, Matthew and Dennis. *Deliverance Prayer: Experiential, Psychological, and Theological Approaches*. New York: Paulist Press, 1981.

Lloyd-Jones, D. Martyn. *The Christian Soldier: An Exposition of Ephesians 6:10–20*. Grand Rapids: Baker, 1977.

————. *The Christian Warfare: An Exposition of Ephesians 6:10–13.* Grand Rapids: Baker, 1976.

Martin, Walter. *Kingdom of the Cults.* Minneapolis: Bethany, 1965.

Metcalf, J. C. *The Great Enemy.* Dorset, England: Overcomer Literature Trust, n.d.

Michaelson, Johanna. *The Beautiful Side of Evil.* Eugene, Ore.: Harvest House, 1982.

Montgomery, John Warwick. *Principalities and Powers.* Minneapolis: Bethany House, 1973.

Peck, M. Scott. *People of the Lie: The Hope for Healing Human Evil.* New York: Simon & Schuster, 1983.

Penn-Lewis, Jessie. *War on the Saints.* Fort Washington, Pa.: Christian Literature Crusade, 1977 (original edition, 1912).

Scanlan, Michael and Randall J. Cirner. *Deliverance from Evil Spirits.* Ann Arbor, Mich.: Servant Books, 1980.

Smith, F. LaGuard. *Out on a Broken Limb.* Eugene, Ore.: Harvest House, 1985.

Stedman, Ray C. *Spiritual Warfare: Winning the Daily Battle with Satan.* Portland: Multnomah, 1975.

Swindoll, Charles R. *Demonism: How to Win Against the Devil.* Portland: Multnomah, 1981.

Unger, Merrill. *Demons in the World Today.* Wheaton, Ill.: Tyndale, 1971.

Usher, Charles H. *Satan: A Defeated Foe.* Fort Washington, Pa.: Christian Literature Crusade, n.d.

Wiersbe, Warren W. *The Strategy of Satan: How to Detect and Defeat Him.* Wheaton: Tyndale, 1979.

Reference Works and Exegetical Studies

Abbot-Smith, G. *A Manual Greek Lexicon of the New Testament.* New York: Charles Scribner's Sons, n.d.

Aland, Kurt, *et. al.* eds. *The Greek New Testament.* Stuttgart, W. Germany: United Bible Societies, 1968.

Brown, Colin, ed. *Dictionary of New Testament Theology,* 3 vols. Grand Rapids: Zondervan, 1978.

Harris, R. Laird, ed. *Theological Wordbook of the Old Testament,* 2 vols. Chicago: Moody, 1980.

Kittel, Gerhard and Friedrich, Gerhard, eds. *Theological Dictionary of the New Testament,* abridged in one volume by Geoffrey Bromiley. Grand Rapids: Eerdmans/Paternoster, 1985.

Nicoll, W. Robertson, ed. *The Expositor's Greek Testament,* 5 vols. Grand Rapids: Eerdmans, 1974.

Robertson, A. T. *Word Pictures in the Greek New Testament,* 6 vols. Nashville: Broadman, 1930.

Sturz, Henry. *The Byzantine Text Type in New Testament Textual Criticism.* Nashville: Thomas Nelson, 1984.

Thayer, Joseph Henry. *Thayer's Greek-English Lexicon of the New Testament.* Grand Rapids: Zondervan, 1973.

Other Books

Bonhoeffer, Dietrich. *Letters and Papers from Prison.* New York: Macmillan, Collier Books, 1972.

Brueggemann, Walter. *Genesis.* Atlanta: John Knox Press, 1982.

Dawson, John. *Taking Our Cities for God: How to Break Spiritual Stongholds.* Altamonte Springs, Fla.: Creation House, 1989.

Dunn, James D. G. *Jesus and the Spirit.* Philadelphia: Westminster, 1975.

Ells, Al. *One Way Relationships.* Nashville: Thomas Nelson, 1990.

Erickson, Millard J. *Christian Theology,* Vol. I. Grand Rapids: Baker, 1983.

Foster, Richard. *The Celebration of Discipline.* New York: Harper & Row, 1978.

Green, Michael. *I Believe in the Holy Spirit.* Grand Rapids: Eerdmans, 1975.

Kinnaman, Gary D. *And Signs Shall Follow.* Old Tappan, N.J.: Chosen Books, 1987.

Kraft, Charles. *Christianity with Power.* Ann Arbor, Mich.: Servant Books, 1989.

Law, Terry. *The Power of Praise and Worship.* Tulsa: Victory House, 1985.

Moody, D. L. *Secret Power.* Chicago: Moody Press, n.d.

Murray, Andrew. *The Ministry of Intercession*. Springdale, Pa.:
Whitaker House, 1982.

Peterson, Eugene. *Earth and Altar*. Downers Grove, Ill.: Inter-
Varsity, 1984.

Pytches, David. *Spiritual Gifts in the Local Church*. Minneapolis:
Bethany, 1985.

Powell, John. *Why Am I Afraid to Tell You Who I Am?* Chicago:
Argus, 1969.

Smail, Thomas. *Reflected Glory: The Spirit in Christ and Christians*.
Grand Rapids: Eerdmans, 1975.

Snyder, Howard. *Foresight: Ten Major Trends that Will Dramatically Affect the Future of the Church*. Nashville: Thomas Nelson, 1986.

Torrey, R. A. *The Power of Prayer*. Grand Rapids: Zondervan,
1968.

Wagner, C. Peter. *Your Spiritual Gifts Can Help Your Church Grow*.
Ventura, Cal.: Regal, 1979.

Watson, David. *Called and Committed: World-Changing Discipleship*. Wheaton, Ill.: Harold Shaw, 1982.

Weber, Otto. *Foundations of Dogmatics*, Vol. I. Grand Rapids:
Eerdmans, 1981.

Periodicals and Other Articles

Ford, Ron. "The Powerful Advance of God's Kingdom in the
Earth." *First Fruits*. January/February 1986, pp. 16–18.

Kraft, Charles. "Shifting World Views, Shifting Attitudes."
Equipping the Saints. September/October 1987, pp. 10–12.

Mollen, Art. "Prayer Contributes to Health." *Arizona Republic*.
December 1988, Classified Section, p. 1.

Smith, F. LaGuard. "There Is No God But You." *The Wittenburg
Door*. March/April 1989, pp. 16 *ff*.

Wagner, C. Peter. "The Power of Corporate Prayer." *Ministries
Today*, September/October 1989, p. 28.

———. "Territorial Spirits," an unpublished manuscript from
the Academic Symposium on Power Evangelism, Fuller
Seminary, December 13–15, 1988.

Index

Scripture Index